Daily Dress at Deir el-Medîna

Words for Clothing

Jac. J. Janssen

Golden House Publications

Egyptology 8

London 2008

This title is published by
Golden House Publications

Printed in the United Kingdom
by

T J International Ltd
Trecerus Industrial Estate
PADSTOW
Cornwall PL28 8RW

London 2008

ISBN 13: 978-1-906137-05-2
ISBN 10: 1-906137-05-6

Contents

Picture source:
Cover: B. Bruyère, *Rapport sur les Fouilles de Deir el Médineh (1934-1935)*, Deuxième Partie: La nécropole de l'est (Le Caire 1937), 62, fig. 32
Page vi: E. Schiaparelli, *La tomba intatta dell' architetto Cha nella necropoli di Tebe* (Turin, 1927), 94, fig. 64

Acknowledgements

This volume has come to fruition due to the efforts of three people. I must firstly thank my publisher Dr. Wolfram Grajetzki of Golden House Publications. I am most grateful for the considerable amount of the time and effort that he has expended on the process. I much admire his unfailing willingness and good humour in hand delivering sets of proofs to my home.

My wife Rosalind Janssen typed the bulk of the text from my barely legible handwritten manuscript, taking time away from her own studies in order to do so. The various tables are the work of Luciana Carvalho; I am most grateful for her willingness to help with both this and subsequent manuscripts.

Unlike my great mentor Sir Alan Gardiner, I am not yet prepared to say that this volume is my swan song. Despite the fact that it will be published in my eighty-sixth year, there are already three further contributions to Deir el-Medîna studies that now await publication

Jac. J. Janssen February 2008

A pile of fifty triangular loincloths from the tomb of Kha (note his laundry mark).

Chapter 1

Introduction

> *Texts and archaeology each give, in their own different ways, incomplete pictures of pre-modern societies. Where the two exist in parallel they often do not dovetail easily together …… Only by constant confrontation of the two, and an acceptance that they have equal weight but require different responses, can a fuller picture of the past be obtained.*
>
> B. Kemp and G. Vogelsang-Eastwood, *The Ancient Textile Industry at Amarna*, p. 476.

The question to which the present study attempts to give an answer is: what clothes did the people wear during the New Kingdom? Not the Pharaohs or the high officials, the upper ten, but ordinary workmen and their families. Whether that was also the way the peasants were dressed is uncertain; what those people were wearing is not the subject of what follows.

The only community of workmen from which we possess sufficient evidence to try and find the answer to the question is that of the inhabitants of Deir el-Medîna, the settlement of the necropolis workmen of the West Bank of Thebes. From the thousands of ostraca preserved from there, plus a number of papyri, we are able to collect enough material for at least a partial answer. That it is far from complete will become clear. However, texts contain only words. The Egyptian writing may usually show, by adding to a word the determinative V6 (𓍱), that it indicates an object consisting of cloth; this does not help us in discovering what kind of garment was meant, For that the word needs to be used in a sentence (not in a list) which tells us how the garment was worn.

On the other hand, a few actual clothes of the workmen have been found, although not enough to help us much further. More important are the representations on the tomb-walls of the community. At least, if we could be certain that they indeed depict the people in their normal dress. Unfortunately, that is far from clear.[1]

Finally, there are the so-called "pictorial clothing lists" on ostraca, which seem to contain valuable data. In how far all this together leads to more or less definite answers we will see below.

The main subject of what follows is neither the discussion of the names of the various articles of dress, extensive as it will be, for Egyptologists are as yet not at all certain in these matters[2]; nor is it that of the actual garments or that of the clothes shown in the tomb scenes, but the relations between these categories: what kind of garment is meant by a particular word, and how was a particular piece of dress called.[3] As Kemp and Vogelsang-Eastwood in their study of *The Ancient Textile Industry at Amarna* state (p. 438): "...... the grounds for identifying most of [the words] in term of garment types are generally weak." That is, however, no reason not to try to strengthen them as good as we can.

From the outset one point has to be kept in mind: many Egyptian garments, perhaps the majority, were not tailored.[4] They consist simply of rectangular pieces of cloth of various lengths and widths which were wrapped around (parts of) the body in different ways. Therefore it is many times unclear which aspect led to the name of a particular item of dress.[5] The result is, as we will see, that several details remain vague. Yet, it seems to me useful to put together what we (think to?) know, as the point of departure for further research.

That this is not superfluous becomes clear when one looks up the translations of various words for clothes in recent dictionaries.[6] Lesko's *A Dictionary of Late Egyptian*, for instance, translates *ifd* (vol. I, p. 30) as "sheet, garment (piece of linen)", and *mss* (vol. I, p. 242) as "apron, kilt, tunic". These renderings exclude each other, while the translation of *sḏ* (vol. III, p. 123; actually, as the hieroglyphic forms noted at the right-hand side of the page show, mostly *sḏy*, less frequently *sḏw*, and twice *sḏwy*) as "*sdy*-garment"[7] is not very satisfactory.

Rainer Hannig, in his recent *Grosses Handwörterbuch Ägyptisch-Deutsch*, is mostly less vague, but both *rwḏ* (p. 463)[8] and *ḫnkt* (p. 638) are rendered as "e. Kleidungsstück"; that is, they are actually left untranslated. For *dꜣiw* (p. 969) Hannig notes: "(1) Leinenstoffballen" and "(2) (grosser) Schurz, Kilt; Galabiye, Umhang". The first will be correct for texts older than the New Kingdom, but that a garment could be indicated by a word that means as well "kilt" as "ghalabiya", that is, a piece of cloth covering only the lower part of the body as well as one covering the entire body, looks at least unlikely.[9]

All this is not the fault of the editors of these dictionaries; it reflects the situation in Egyptology. Evidently, a fair bit of study and discussion is still needed. For that reason it seems useful to present a picture of the level of knowledge we have reached today. In so doing it is necessary to keep in mind that our modern words for various garments are not always unambiguous. For instance: if indeed *rwḏw* is a piece of cloth worn over the tunic, as representations show (see below, p. 39), and is mostly pleated, how should we call it? Is it a "shawl", as I have once suggested, or rather a "sash"[10]; or should we call it an "apron"?

It is also good not to forget that a particular garment may be known under different names. That could depend upon the person who wears it, whether a woman or a man, as in our language the pair “skirt / kilt” shows.[11] It may also depend upon the circumstances in which the garment is worn. What in everyday life is called a lady’s “dress” can be indicated as “frock” or even “gown”. Incidentally it can be difficult to see why a particular word is used and not its equivalent, such as in the pair “shirt / blouse”. That means that, even if we find two Egyptian words which seem to indicate the same item of dress, this is not necessarily wrong.

One more aspect requires at least to be mentioned, namely: how did the inhabitants of Deir el-Medîna acquire the clothes they did wear? Partly they were received among the deliveries by which the government paid for the work in the royal tomb. That garments constituted an essential part of these “wages” appears evident from the complaints uttered during the strikes in year 29 of Ramesses III. The first thing the workmen are said to miss were their *ḥbs.w*, “clothes”.[12] Also in year 3 of Ramesses IV, when the men appealed to the officials to pay their “wages”, the first category mentioned was *p3y.sn ḥbs.w*, “their clothes”.[13]

There are also a few texts which record the actual delivery of garments; e.g., O. DeM 406, which lists the men to whom a garment was distributed, or O. DeM 10019, 4, where we read that, on a specific day (IV *3ḫt* 11) when the crew did not work (*wsf*), garments were distributed. This text dates from the very end of the reign of Ramesses IV or the beginning of that of Ramesses V.[14] From year 16 of Ramesses IX dates Pap. Turin 2004 + 2007 + 2057/58 + 2106/396, which tells us that, on IV *3ḫt* 18, “the garments” (*n3 ḥbs.w*) were received,[15] while on the next day “the garments of the crew” were received in the House of Ma‘at by the vizier.[16] They are recorded in detail: the five superiors got each a *dw*, 61 men each one *rwḏw*, the two doorkeepers together 2 *rwḏw*, the guardian 8 *rwḏw* and 9 *dw* (!).[17]

This is rather a late text for Deir el-Medîna, but still later, from year 4-5 of the *wḥm-mswt* Era is Pap. Turin 1903, where in vs. II, 18-19 it is stated that no less than 253 *rwḏw.w* were received, as well as the same number of *mss.w.*[18] Why so many is not clear, but at least this text and the other ones prove that clothing was received from the State. Perhaps only clothes for men;[19] for their wives and children yarn was distributed as part of the wages, which was made into clothes in the community itself. However, it was perhaps not all that was needed. The workmen sometimes acquired yarn, possibly also clothes, from outside (see below, p. 12).

As for the evidence on which this study is based, that is mainly found in the ostraca from Deir el-Medîna, papyri from that place not being really numerous. Among the ostraca one category is particularly important for the subject, namely those with lists of clothes, in some cases interspaced by a name or the word for house (*pr*) plus a name (e.g. O.DeM 258). At least 15 of such ostraca have been preserved.[20]

Notes

1) See my remarks on this aspect in *Commodity Prices*, 249-251.
2) Cf. Valbelle, *Les Ouvriers*, 281.
3) The problems of the nomenclature were consciously excluded by Gillian Vogelsang-Eastwood from her fundamental study *Pharaonic Egyptian Clothing* (Leiden, 1993); see her p. 8. However, on p. 183, in the very last sentence, she notes: "...... there are many potential areas of future research, not the least of which is the matching together of known types of textiles and clothing with the written Egyptian terminology."

4) Cf. e.g. Rita Freed in *Egypt's Golden Age. The Art of Living in the New Kingdom* (Boston, 1982), 170.
5) See e.g. below, p. 27.
6) Cf. also Valbelle, *Les ouvriers*, 281-283.
7) Why the meaning of *sḏ* (with a *ḏ*) is said to be "*sdy*-garment" (with a *d*) is a mystery.
8) That *šmꜥ* is here translated as "oberägyptisches" and *nꜥꜥ* as "weiches" are slips. On p. 821 *šmꜥt* is correctly said to be "e. Leinenart", while on p. 95 *nꜥꜥ* is stated to mean i.a. "glatt, fein".
   To "e. Kleidungstück" is added between brackets "Schal". Does that way of presenting it mean that this rendering is uncertain?
9) See also, for various translations of *dꜣỉw*, *Commodity Prices*, 265.
10) *Commodity Prices*, 284.
11) In O. DeM 587, 6 Wente translates (*Letters*, nr. 219, p. 154) *dꜣỉꜣ* a "skirt", for this is a letter by Paser to a woman called Tutuia. In other instances, where the garment is that of a man, he renders the word as "kilt"; e.g. O. DeM 131, vs. 1 (*Letters*, nr. 249, p. 161), O. Petrie 82, 4 (*Letters*, nr. 240, p. 159), or. O. Černý 19, vs. 3 (*Letters*, nr. 218, p. 153).
12) Turin Strike Papyrus (Pap. Turin 1880), rt. 2, 3 (*RAD* 53, 16).
13) Pap. DeM XXIV (Černý, *Pap. hiératiques de Deir el-Médineh* II, pl. 9), 1 ; cf. Eyre, *GM* 98 (1987), 13.
14) So Gutgesell, *Die Datierung der Ostraka und Papyri aus Deir el-Medineh*, Teil I, Band II, 385 (O. DeM 10019 was formerly known as O. IFAO 1244).
15) Rt. 2, 1 (K*RI* VI, 650).
16) Rt. 2, 6 (K*RI* VI, 651).

17) In verso Text A, 1 (K*RI* VI, 652) we read: "Amount (*ʿḥʿ*) of the garments given to us: 70 *mss* garments" (sic! *ḥbs.w mss*).
18) K*RI* VII, 396.
19) Cf. Valbelle, *Les ouvriers*, 152. See also p. 249.
20) They are: O. DeM 86 (col. II), 87, 88, 90, 210, 211, 212 (col. I), 258, 341 (recto), 404, 452, 583, 924, 10067 (= O. AG 110).

Chapter 2

General Remarks

It may be useful, before discussing the various names of garments as they appear in Deir el-Medîna texts, to pay attention to the words which denote the condition and fabric of the clothes, as well as a few other general aspects.

A term which occurs several times in the lists (see Chapter 5), but also elsewhere, is *ỉswt* ( ), also written *ỉsy* ( ),[1] which means "old, worn out (clothes)" → "rags". The word *ỉs*(*w*) occurs as well as an adjective after the name of a garment, e.g. in O. DeM 90, 3: *dw ỉs* ( ) and line 6: *sḏw*[2] *ỉs*, or in O. Varille 19, I, 4 and 5: *sḏwy ỉswt* ( ) and *dꜣỉꜣ*[3] *ỉswt* ( ). Another way of stating the same occurs, e.g. in O. Černý 19 (= *Hier. Ostr.* 54/4), vs. 2-4: *pꜣy ỉsw n dꜣỉꜣ ḥnʿ pꜣy ỉsw n sḏỉꜣ*.[3] In O. DeM 790, vs. 2, Grandet reads (p. 62): [*ḏꜣ*]*j* (?) *js jw šʿd* (= *w*) *ḥr.f*,[4] translating it as: "un vieux vêtement [*dja*]*y*, dont l'extrémité a été coupée". I wonder whether *ḥr* means here not rather "front" or "top".

This ostracon brings us to another word indicating that the garment was in a bad state; viz. *šʿd*. That word occurs, apart from here (where it is by exception fully written out as), also e.g. in O. BM 50737, 5 (*sḏy*).[5] *šʿd* means "to fell, to cut down (trees)", "to cut off", and suchlike. In the case of clothes it seems to be: "to tear, to mutilate".

Then there is *thm*, which appears in O. Berlin P 12649, 3 (written) and in Pap. Turin 1885, vs. II, 6 (= K*RI* VI, 71) as , both times with *rwḏw*. Although in these instances the *m* is not written out, there can hardly be any doubt about the reading. In O. Gardiner 67 (= Hier. Ostr. 47/2), 4, the *m* is noted: *ỉw bn sw* (a *ẖnk*) . Also in O. DeM 923, 3 (a *dw*).[6] The general meaning is "damaged", perhaps in the case of clothes "with holes".

These three words, *ỉs*, *šꜥd* and *thm*, are the opposite of *ḳn* or *n ḳn*, which is several times added to all kinds of words for garments.[7] Hannig, *Grosses Handwörterbuch*, 859, states that it indicates the best quality of the material, but I would rather suggest that it describes the state of the garment. Hence I translate it as "in perfect condition". In Pap. Chester Beatty III, vs. 5, 2, there are written after each other, *dw*, *rwḏw*, and *sḏw*, each said to be *n ḳn*. Gardiner renders it (p. 25) as "finest", but that seems to be not quite what it means. Finally, a clear case is found in the recently discussed O. Gardiner 219[8] + O. BM 25289, 8 (cf. *JEA* 90, 2004, 217): ...... *n ḳn dꜣỉw ỉsw m ky* .... Haring translates: "...... (?) in good condition, a worn-out skirt, being (?) another [......]". One could also suggest: "...... in good condition, one[9] *dꜣỉw*; worn-out in (??) another (sc. *dꜣỉw*)".[10]

In some papyri – so far as I know nowhere in an ostracon – the name of a garment is preceded by or followed by *m* . This happens, for instance, in Pap. BM 10068, II, 13 (with *mss*) and in line 22 (with *ỉdg*), both times preceded by *mk* (for this word, see below, p. 14); in Pap. Bibliothèque Nationale 197, V, 3-4 (= Černý, *Late Ramesside Letters*, 35): *ḥbsw ỉs m*  *ḳnw*; and in Pap. Leiden I 352, 9 (= *JEA* 23, 1937, 186): *šmꜥ nfr mss.tỉ* [sic] . Wente, *Late Ramesside Letters*, p. 53, discusses our second instance, reading it as *m ꜥrk*. However, Sturtewagen in *Studies in Egyptology* (FS Miriam Lichtheim), vol. II, 939, discussing  *twt* in the Turin Strike Papyrus (= Pap. Turin 1880), vs. 5, 18 (*RAD* 48, 6), argues, certainly correctly, that  means *sfḫ*. He renders this instance as "used sandals”. Černý translated the instance in the Leiden papyrus – reading it also as *m sfḫ* – with “cast off”. When occurring with tools, I have argued (*Commodity Prices*, 312, note 4) that it means “blunt”. Generally, it apparently indicates an object that has become obsolete and therefore should be removed.

Sometimes the name of a garment is followed by the word *sḫt*, “woven”,[11] or *nbd*, “plaited”, once a *mss* is even said to be *ḫnd*, “twined”.[12] *sḫt* occurs e.g. in O. BM 5643 (= *Hier. Ostr.* 85/2), 6-7: *sḏw sḫt* (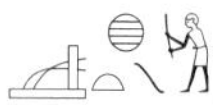) *ỉr.n ḫꜣr* 1, *rwḏw sḫt* 1 *ỉr.n ḫꜣr* ¾. Both prices are below the usual level. Other instances of *sḫt* are: O. DeM 428 vs.: *ḥtrỉ n ỉsh sḫ.ty*; O. DeM 183, 3: *dꜣiꜣ*[3] *sḫt* 1 *ỉr.n ḫꜣr* 2; O. Gardiner 166, 7 (= Allam, *Hieratische Ostraka und Papyri,* 46 and K*RI* III, 550); *rwḏw sḫt*. Why is that *sḫt* added in these instances? That garments are made from woven textiles is rather obvious. Weaving is even a few times explicitly recorded in the ostraca.[13] Why then mention it, and why is the price in these cases lower than ususal?[14] That suggests that *sḫt* indicates here something special, a particular type of fabric perhaps. The word alone (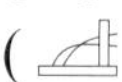), written in red, occurs in the Gurob Fragments (*RAD* 24, 15 = Fragment Y1, 12 and 25, 13 = Y2, 11[15]). Evidently, in our texts it does not mean top quality. Was that because the garments were made of cloth woven at home, hence less good than normal?

The word *nbd*[16] is so far as I know only once written before the word for a garment, namely in O. Cairo 25585, 3: *nbd mss* 1 *ỉr.n dbn* 5 (the usual price!), on which follows: *kty ỉr.n dbn* 3, “another (sc. *mss*) worth 3 *deben*”. In O. DeM 131, vs. 1, the author of the letter states: *ỉw.i nbd* [sic!] 2 *dw*, adding in the next line that he did *tp*, “stitch”,[17] a tunic and a *ḥtrỉ n ỉsh*. Wente (*Letters*, nr. 249) translates the first line as “I shall weave two kilts”, as if *sḫt*, not *nbd*, was written.[18] Kemp and Vogelsang-Eastwood, however, suggested[19] that *nbd* (or *tpỉ*) could perhaps mean "to add pleats". For *tpỉ* that looks to me very unlikely, but for *nbd* it may be possible.

Quite a different kind of addition to a word for garment is the phrase *n Pr-ꜥꜣ ꜥ.w.s.* This occurs, for example, with *mss* in O. Gardiner 103 (= *Hier. Ostr.* 52/2), vs. B 9, and in O. DeM 931, 3; with *rwḏw* in O. Gardiner 265, 2; with *sḏw* in O. DeM 929, 4; with *dꜣỉw* in O. Gardiner 265, 4. What does it mean that clothes are explicitly stated to be "of Pharaoh l.p.h."? In O. Petrie 18 (= *Hier. Ostr.* 70/1), 5, there is said: *šsp.sw* [= *.s*] *pꜣ dw ỉ.dỉ n.ỉ pꜣ Pr-ꜥꜣ ꜥ.w.s*, "She received the kilt (skirt) which the Pharaoh l.p.h. gave me". This stress on the fact that it was Pharaoh who gave it makes the impression that this was not self-evident. In Pap. Geneva D 191, vs. 18-19 (= Černý, *Late Ramesside Letters*, 60) we read about the god's father Esamenope "whom Pharaoh l.p.h. has clothed (*ḥbsw*) with a tunic as is fitting (*m šꜣỉw*)". Again, it is explicitly stated that Pharaoh did it. Was this unusual? Were the majority of the clothes worn by the workmen not part of the deliveries by the State, i.e. Pharaoh, as their "wages"? As on so many points, when we try to follow the details of daily life in Ancient Egypt, even in the community of necropolis workmen about which we know so much, we soon hit the limits of our knowledge.

Another aspect of clothes which should be discussed here is that of the material of which they were made. So far as we know this was always linen, in various qualities. These are indicated by three terms: *nꜥꜥ*,[20] *šmꜥ*,[21] and *šmꜥ nfr.*[22] Usually they are translated as "smooth", "thin", and "fine/good thin". The word "smooth" looks to be in this context a euphemism; it was the cheapest quality.

Which of the three was mostly used in the community? In many instances we do not know the fabric since it was not noted. Of the 94 ostraca in which *mss* occurs, together 112 times, only 53 mention the fabric: of the 89 ostraca where *dꜣỉw* occurs, together 110 times, only 25 record the material.[23] For some other pieces of dress, e.g. *ỉsh*, *pyr*, *mrw* and *ẖnk*, we have little or no evidence.[24] The bandage *pyr* is described in O. DeM 187, 5-6 as consisting of *ỉnsy*, "red cloth", and in O. Turin 57366, vs. 2 as *dgꜣ m nwb*, "decked with gold", but that is exceptional. Moreover, it is no indication of its fabric.

The material of which each item of dress usually consisted is the following:

ỉfd. Mostly *nꜥꜥ*, which is mentioned more than half the number of texts (28 out of 53): *šmꜥ* and *šmꜥ nfr* are rare.

ỉdg. In itself not common (only 18 times in 14 ostraca, and 9 in 7 papyri); it is stated to be of *šmꜥ* (10 times) and *šmꜥ nfr* (4 times); only once of *nꜥꜥ*.

mss. Like *dꜣỉw* it is recorded over a hundred times, usually said to consist of *nꜥꜥ*, seldom of *šmꜥ* or *šmꜥ nfr*. It was evidently a fairly strong garment, protecting the body against high and low temperatures.

rwḏw. This garment occurs rather frequently in our texts; I found it 110 times in 66 ostraca and papyri. It is not seldom said to be made of *šmꜥ*, which is not surprising if it was a shawl. Yet, the eleven instances of it are still less than the 38 where it consisted of *nꜥꜥ* (16 in Pap. BM 10068, vs. I).

sḏw / *sḏy*. I found this only very slightly less times than *mss* (122 in 88 texts). It is relatively frequently stated to be of *šmꜥ* (6 times) or *šmꜥ nfr* (5 times) which, if it was used at the loins, is understandable. Yet, about a dozen times it is said to consist of *nꜥꜥ* cloth.

dꜣỉw. This common garment (143 times mentioned) was about as many times recorded as being made of each of the three kinds of fabric. In about 28% of the instances the type of cloth is stated, less than *mss* (47%).

ḏꜣyt. This type of garment is noted 48 times in our material. In almost half the instances a particular fabric is mentioned, mostly *nꜥꜥ*, as one would expect of a cloak.

All together *nʿʿ* occurs over 165 times, *šmʿ* 50, and *šmʿ nfr* about 30; that is, *nʿʿ* is more common than the other two put together. Moreover, the fabric, especially when of the better quality, is relatively more regularly recorded in the papyri than in the ostraca. For instance, *šmʿ nfr* 4 times for a *dꜣiw* in 21 papyri as against 7 times in 89 ostraca; but, admittedly, the texts on papyrus are mostly longer than those on an average ostracon.

As mentioned above (note 22), there was also a type of cloth called *mk*, which occurs in Pap. BM 10068, II, 13 as the material of two *mss* and in line 22 as that of two *idg*,[25] but so far as I know it never turns up in an ostracon. A few years ago my wife and I published an article on it[26] in which we reached the conclusion that the word means "tapestry weaving"; that is, unlike *nʿʿ* or *šmʿ* - or *sšr-nsw* – not a special quality of thread, but a particular type of weaving, in which extra threads are inserted to create ornamentation. The phrase *sšr-nsw m bꜣkw n mk* in a hieratic inscription from the tomb of Tutankhamun[27] shows the difference from the other terms.

As for an instructive example showing various points mentioned above as well as prices which are discussed below, I quote here the unpublished Pap. Turin 2104/223, vs. II:[28]

4. *nʿʿ d̲ꜣy*	1	*ir.n dbn* 30
5. *nʿʿ d̲ꜣy*	1	*ir.n dbn* 20
6. *nʿʿ ifd*	1	*ir.n dbn* 12
7. *šmʿ dw*	1	*ir.n dbn* 20
8. *nʿʿ sd̲y*	1	*ir.n dbn* 10
9. *nʿʿ mss*	2	*ir.n dbn* 10
10. *šʿd d̲ꜣy*	8	*ir.n dbn* 5
11. *h̯t tbit ḥbsw*[29]	1	*ir.n dbn* 10

What follows are mostly not items of dress.[30]

A few details may be highlighted:

a) all garments are stated to consist of *nʿʿ* except the *dw*, which is of *šmʿ*.

b) whereas a *dꜣy* cost 20 to 30 *deben* (lines 4 and 5), eight of them which are mutilated (*šʿd*), hence rags, cost together only 5 *deben*.

c) the *ỉfd* appears here (line 6) in between garments; does that mean that actually textiles are listed, not clothes, or is this a proof that *ỉfd* could be a garment? See below, p. 22.

An aspect which is present in the papyrus just quoted and which should at least be mentioned is that of the prices of the items of dress. Since I published my *Commodity Prices* in 1975 not much more evidence for it has come to light.[31] The question is here: could the prices help us in identifying the clothes?

In her study *Les ouvriers de la tombe*, Dominique Valbelle expresses her doubt (p. 283, note 3) about my identification of *sḏw* / *sḏy* as "pagne" (loincloth) on account of its prices, which vary from 5 to 20 *deben*.[32] Recently Barry Kemp and Gillian Vogelsang-Eastwood, in their book *The Ancient Textile Industry of Amarna*, raised doubt (p. 442) on the generally acknowledged rendering of *mss* as "tunic", also on account of the prices. Whereas a *mss* cost almost always 5 *deben*, a *sḏw* / *sḏy* "loincloth", costs two or three times as much, and that, as they argue, while one could make at least three loincloths out of one tunic. One could for a moment think that the material was the cause of the difference, but we know for instance that a *dꜣỉw* of *nʿʿ* cost 20 *deben* (O. IFAO 764, Left),[33] the same price as some others made of *šmʿ*.

This is not the place to try to solve the problem. One thing may be clear: the prices do not really help us to identify various words for garments; on the contrary.

Finally, quite a different aspect which the study of the words for items of dress brings to light is the following. The word for "kilt" or "skirt", *dꜣ ỉw* – so it appears in dictionaries –

is in the ostraca many times written as *dw*, but it occurs also as *dꜣỉꜣ*, with an *ꜣ* instead of the final *w*. In that case – seldom when the ending is an *w* – the determinative can be , an alternative for alone. I know this of nine ostraca,[34] for instance, O. Petrie 82 (= *Hier. Ostr.* 35/2), 4; O. Černý 19 (= *Hier. Ostr.* 54/4), vs. 3 and 4; O. DeM 30, 5; O. DeM 283, 1; O. Varille 19, I, 2 and 5. When the determinative is a simple the final *ꜣ* is found even more frequently. A few examples are: O. Gardiner 8 (= *Hier. Ostr.* 31/5), 1; O. DeM 183, 3 (*dꜣỉꜣ sẖt*); O. Gardiner 265, 4 (*dꜣỉꜣ n Pr-ꜥꜣ ꜥ.w.s*); the Lady Franklin Hieratic Inscription (= K*RI* VII, 341), 3. There occurs also more than once a defective writing of *dꜣỉw* without the first *ꜣ* ( ), e.g. O. Gardiner 139, 6; O. Černý 20, 4 (= K*RI* VII, 344); O. DeM 552, 1 (; in line 4).

The final aleph in *dꜣỉꜣ* can be compared with the *ꜣ* in *ỉshꜣ*, a form of *ỉsh* which occurs almost as frequently as that without the aleph. More peculiar is, in O. DeM 258, the form (with !) for *sḏy*, which appears in lines 5, 6 and 7 – and perhaps also in line 8, now mostly lost. The same form turns up in O. Černý 19 (= *Hier. Ostr.* 54/4), vs. 4 and 5,[35] hence in more than one text, so probably not a slip of the pen. Moreover, in that O. DeM 258 we find also, in lines 3 and 7, the even more conspicuous form for *ẖnk*, a spelling which is perhaps also found in O. DeM 88, 3.

A provisional conclusion of these data could be: there existed – with some Deir el- Medîna scribes? – a vague inclination to end words for garments on a *ꜣ*. Or: the fairly common form *dꜣỉꜣ* influenced the spelling of other names of clothes. But why *dꜣỉꜣ* for *dꜣỉw* / *dw*?

Notes

1. E.g. in O. Turin 57464, 2. In O. Vienna 1 (*JEA* 65, 1979, 90), 5: . In O. Strasbourg H 87.2 it is simply written , without . A problem is   in O. Cairo 25819, 3. In my *Ship's Logs* (p. 31) I once, hesitatingly, translated "(shabby dresses?) [made of?] *ỉsy* (rushes)". Helck, *Materialien*, 813 rejects that rendering ("Sicherlich ist es nicht"), I think now correctly. But what is then meant by the second *ỉsy*? "Old" rags seems not very convincing.
2. In Černý's transcription , but see below, p. 47. The word *ỉs* is here used in contrast to the preceding *ḳn*. For this word, see below.
3. For the spelling with an *ȝ,* see p. 16.
4. Grandet ignores what he himself transcribed on p. 191 as (below ), and refers for the writing to O. DeM 558, 2. Does he mean that  should be transcribed as  and not as ?
5. This *sḏy* costs 4 *deben*, which is less than normal (cf. *Commodity Prices*, 275), as one would expect for a torn garment.
6. Grandet translates here "troué" (with holes).
7. In O. Berlin P 12649: *ḳn mss*, *ḳn ỉsh*, and *ḳn mrw*; in O. Nash 3 (= *Hier. Ostr.* 56/2), 3: *n ḳn mss*; in O. Gardiner 233, 4: *n ḳn ỉfd n*[ʿʿ]; see also note 2 above.
8. Now O. Ashmolean Museum 219, as Haring correctly calls it.
9. The stroke after *dȝỉw* is the figure.
10. In both translations the exact rendering of *m* is problematic.

11. In *Ancient Egyptian Materials and Technology*, ed. by Nicholson and Shaw, chapter 11, Gillian Vogelsang-Eastwood describes (pp. 274-276) various techniques of weaving, without mentioning the Egyptian terms for them.
12. O. Gardiner 190, vs. 7: *pꜣ ḫndy tꜣ ms*[*s*].
13. O. DeM 49, 3: "Given to him in exchange for the coffin: weaving (*sḫty*) *wꜥ dꜣỉw ỉr.n snỉw* 3". In O. DeM 132, 3: "And she wove for me this *rwḏw*". Such sentences show that garments were woven in the Village itself. So too in O. AG 53, vs. 4: *dỉ.tn sḫt.sn tꜣ mss*, "You let them weave the tunic". Note that one weaves a garment, not the cloth of it.
14. In O. DeM 925, 2 we read: *mss šrỉt r sḫt bty ỉpt* 2. Grandet (p. 101, note 2) explains the *r* before *sḫt* (also in line 4) as standing for the prothetic yodh of the participle. The price, 2 *oipě*, is abnormally low for a *mss*, but could be due to its small size.
15. For this *sḫt*, see also Posener-Kriéger, *Les archives du temple funéraire de Néferirkarê-Kakaï* (*Les Papyrus d'Abousir*), II, 343-345.
16. *nbd* is the term for coiling, a technique used in the manufacture of basketry; cf. *Commodity Prices*, 136-139. More general: "plaiting".
17. For *tp*, see Černý, *Ägyptologische Studien* (FS Grapow), 33.
18. So too (after Wente?) Mario Tosi and Maria Teresa Nicola, *Vita quotidiana nel villagio operaio di Deir el Medina* (2003), 37: "Io tesserò due gonnellini".
19. *The Ancient Textile Industry of Amarna* (London 2001), 444.
20. That this is as the sign 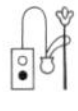 should be read when used with textiles appears evident, for instance, from O.

Berlin P 12647, 2 (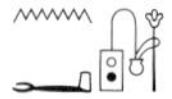) or Pap. Chester Beatty V, 8, 3.

21. The word *šmʿ* is mostly written , sometimes as 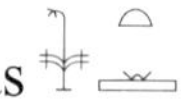.
22. The quality *sšr-nsw*, “royal linen”, also rendered as “byssus” (βύσσος) does not occur in the Deir el-Medîna texts. It was probably too expensive for the workmen. For *mk*, see note 26.
23. For the frequency the material of each garment is noted in ostraca and papyri, see Table I (p. 58).
24. *h̠nk* is also once said to be of *nʿʿ*: O. Berlin P 12649, 3 (*nʿʿ h̠k* [sic] *šrỉ* 2).
25. It is also mentioned with some garments in the Endowment Stela from Thebes (K*RI* II, 710, line x + 6).
26. “*mk.* An Obscure Designation of Cloth” (*LingAeg* 7, 2000, 177-182).
27. In Černý’s publication § 46.
28. The prices are quoted in my *Commodity Prices*. The papyrus dates from the mid-Twentieth Dynasty.
29. “Wooden chest for garments.” Note that the price is for the chest, not for its contents.
30. In col. III, line 2, two pairs of sandals are said to cost 3 *deben*; in line 9 again a *dw* for 20 *deben*. The other items in this column are wooden and metal objects, a hide, and some grain.
31. Some texts were then not yet published, for instance:

    O. Turin 57061, in which three garments of *nʿʿ* quality are recorded: two *sd̠y*, one of 12 *deben* and one of 30 *deben*, and a *rwd̠w* of 15 *deben*. For the fourth garment, perhaps again a *rwd̠w*, no price was noted;

    O. Turin 57349, in which (vs. 5) a *mss* is stated to cost 5 *deben*;

O. DeM 765, 4, where a *ḏꜣy* of *nʿʿ* is valued at 17 *deben*; in line 5 a *dw* of *šmʿ* is noted as costing 15 *deben*, while the price of two *mss* in line 6 is lost; O. BM 50711, 2, with a *mss* of *nʿʿ* again at 5 *deben*.

[The publication has by mistake 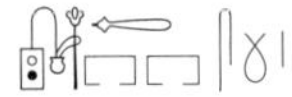, which makes no sense, but see the photograph].

32. See *Commodity Prices*, 275 (Table XLIII).
33. *Commodity Prices*, 266 (Table XLII).
34. From a total of 110 occurrences of this garment in other forms in the ostraca, plus 33 in Deir el-Medîna papyri.
35. Alternating with *dꜣiꜣ*, mentioned above.

Chapter 3

The Common Words for Garments

There are eleven words for items of dress which each occur at least more than ten times in the texts from Deir el-Medîna; sufficient to call them "common". Some I found even up to a hundred times and more; see Table I. Although most of them are well known it seems not superfluous to devote space to their discussion.

ỉfd

The word *ỉfd*, also incidentally written *ỉft*, is known to me from 47 ostraca, in which it occurs 51 times, plus 7 times in 6 papyri from Deir el-Medîna. The name seems to be derived from *ỉfd*, "four", which will imply that it is a square piece of cloth, what we would call a "sheet". It is indeed usually determined by the sign A 55 (), a mummy lying on a bed. I know of only two instances where the sign is absent: O. Turin 57150, 6 () and O. DeM 283, vs. 3 ([1]). Six times I found it written as  only. One of them is O. DeM 769, 3, where it appears at the head of some garments (*r* [*r*]*dỉt rḫ.tw nꜣ ḥbs.w*[2]) of a certain Tatuy. After *ỉfd* follow *dw* and *rwḏw*, all three said to consist of *nʿʿ*. Grandet, in the publication of this text (p. 51), interpreted the sign as *sḏr* and translated it as "matelas", but I doubt whether that can be correct. The object is stated to be of *nʿʿ*, and the word is determined by , whereas *sḏr*, "matrass", is usually written with , being an object made of basketry.[3]

Yet, confusion between *ỉfd* and *sḏr* is not uncommon in the texts. Twice, in O. Cairo 25612, 4 and in O. Berlin P 9408, vs.

4, we read , while in the last text, rt. 4, *ḏr* only is written after *ỉfd* (no *s*). In O. Petrie 48 (= *Hier. Ostr.* 31/4), 2, only an  is inserted between *ỉfd* and the determinative. Moreover, four times there appears  at this place in the word,[4] e.g. in O. Gardiner 123 (= *Hier. Ostr.* 54/1), 5 – but not in line 3! – and in O. Cairo 25583, 2. In O. Cairo 25707, 4, there occurs after *ỉfd* (with ) the word *kꜣr* (), “couch”. All these instances seem to stress that *ỉfd* means “bedsheet”.

On the other hand, in O. DeM 769, quoted above, *ỉfd* is clearly one of the *ḥbs.w*, hence a garment, and that is also the case in other texts.[5] Grandet, in his recent publication of Deir el-Medîna ostraca (vol. X, published in 2006), translates *ỉfd* throughout as “drap”, but in O. DeM 10067 and 10093 rt. it occurs at the end of a list of garments (also in Pap. Chester Beatty V, 8, 3 and Pap. Harris I, 63b, 14), where a bedsheet would not very well fit.

The solution of the problem may be found in a sentence of Bruyère in his *Rapport DeM 1934-1935*, II, p. 58: “Les grandes pièces de lin servaient plutôt de voiles dans lesquels on s’enveloppait par la nuit”. That is, the “sheet” functioned sometimes as a nightdress.[6] Once more we are easily led astray by the meaning words have in our society.

Once an *ỉfd* is called “large” (*ʿꜣ*): in O. DeM 454, vs. I, 7, while in vs. II, 1 five “small” (*šrỉ*) ones are recorded. In 28 instances the material is stated to be *nʿʿ*, ordinary linen; once it is *šmʿ* (Pap. Cairo 65739, 7; cf. *JEA* 21, 1935, pls. XIII-XIV), and twice *šmʿ nfr* (O. Gardiner 133, 2 = K*RI* VII, 182, and Pap. BM 10068, II, 20). The ostracon is an early one, dated to a year 36 which is obviously of Ramesses II.[7] In how far this date could be an explanation of the quality is unclear. Other instances where the material is better than *nʿʿ* occur in papyri;

are they "sheets" from other wardrobes than those of the workmen?

Once, in O. Gardiner 233, 4, the *ỉfd* is said to be *n ḳn*, "in perfect condition". In this instance  is written after *ỉfd* instead of before it, as normally. In Pap. BM 10068, II, 20, we find a rather complex note: *šmꜥ nfr m sfẖ* () *ỉfd m šꜥd* () 2, "two sheets of fine thin cloth, being won out and torn" (see also note 5).

The value of an *ỉfd* is mostly 10 *deben*; cf. *Commodity Prices*, Table XLIX and p. 292. The sheet of Pap. Cairo 65739, the only one of *šmꜥ*, was more than three times as expensive, viz. 3⅓ *kỉte* of silver (= 33 *deben* of copper)

Notes

1. The publication has  , but the *r* is evidently not clear; obviously it should be a *d* or a *t*.
2. Before the word *ḥbs.w* here seems originally to have been written  ; a mistake.
3. For *sḏr*, see *Commodity Prices*, 158-160.
4. The group  may be due to *ỉfdy*, an old word for "couch", which does not anymore occur in the Deir el-Medîna texts.
5. In Pap. BM 10068, II, 20, two *ỉfd.w* are followed, in line 21, by 6, and in line 22, by 2 garments, together called in line 23: *ḥbs.w šbn* 10, "ten various garments". See also Pap. Turin 2104/223, vs. II, 6 (cf. above, p. 14).
6. Cf. also Kemp - Vogelsang-Eastwood, *The Ancient Textile Industry at Amarna*, 441.
7. Černý wrote in his transcription (Notebook 45) the second half of this text in pencil, as if it was hardly legible, but the facsimile by Wimmer (*Hieratische Paläographie der nicht-literarischen Ostraka*, Wiesbaden 1990, Teil I, p. 139) shows the words fairly clearly, in contrast to the beginnings of the lines.

ỉsh

This word I have found in 26 ostraca, together 32 times, but nowhere in any Deir el-Medîna papyrus. Eight times it is part of the expression *ḥtrỉ n ỉsh*. When I wrote the *Commodity Prices*, I had no clear idea what this could mean, but a few years later I suggested that it may be the word for "sleeve" (see *GM* 45, 1981, 21-25), since that would explain why it occurs in pairs (*ḥtrỉ*). Yet, when *ỉsh* alone is written, particularly when the number is one or odd (e.g. in the list of O. DeM 86, II, 6: five) it may be that "pair of sleeves" is also meant.

The word *ỉsh* occurs mainly in lists of garments (15 of the 26 ostraca) and relatively seldom in other texts. It is written either or , but in almost half of the cases an *ꜣ* is added. For this addition, see above, p. 16. The word *ḥtrỉ* is mostly written with M6 ( ) after *ḥtr*, but not in O. DeM 131, vs. 3. The spelling in O. DeM 86, II, 6 (, without or) is exceptional.[1] Even more surprising is the form in O. DeM 363, 2: *ḫtrỉ n* , but Černý seems to have been uncertain about it.[2]

The material of *ỉsh* is nowhere stated, but in O. Prague H 15, 3, the pair is said to be *n ḳn* (written !), "in perfect condition".[3] In O. DeM 428 vs. it is said to be *sḫty*.[4] The sleeves of O. Berlin P 14256, 2 are of a woman (*pꜣy.s ḫtrỉ n ỉshꜣ*).

Once, in O. DeM 283, vs. 1, a *t* is written after the final aleph, as if the word was feminine, but that occurs nowhere else. In O. DeM 363, 1-2, we find *wꜥt* (with a *t* !) *ḥtrỉ n ỉsh*, as if *ḥtrỉ* was feminine, but that expression is twice called *pꜣ*. These *ṯ*s will be mistakes.

Notes

1) Černý noted "sic" above it in his transcription. The use of  instead of  means that it looks somewhat like , "old (clothes)", which also occurs in O. DeM 86, II, in line 8 (this too with "sic" above it).
2) The flower, if indeed that is what is written, is derived from *ỉsw* / *ỉsy*, "reed, rushes".
3) In O. Berlin P 12649, 3a: 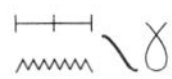 *ỉsh*.
4) The translation of this line by Maren Goecke-Bauer in our *Woodcutters, Potters and Doorkeepers*, (Leiden, 2003), 109, looks not very convincing.

idg

The word *idg* occurs only 18 times in 14 ostraca, and 9 more in 7 papyri. It is throughout written with the ear sign (F 21), in our texts never with a phonetic complement.

I once translated *idg* with "kerchief"[1], the piece of cloth worn over the head. Gillian Vogelsang-Eastwood describes it so: "In general they are made out of a single piece of cloth which was neatened around the edges, but not sewn into a specific shape".[2] Such headgear was not merely worn by workers, even Pharaoh had them,[3] as the many head-cloths of Tutankhamun prove.

However, Edel has argued[4] that *idg* is "Mantel, Umhang" (cloak). His main argument is that in several texts the word directly precedes *mss*, both in the same or about the same numbers[5] so that they seem to form a set. Only once, he notes, does another word for garment come between them.[6] That may be correct, but I fail to see why such a set should consist of a tunic plus a cloak. Why not a tunic and a kerchief?

One of the most illustrative texts in which *idg* is mentioned is O. DeM 1266 + O. Cairo 25218, 20.[7] Max Müller, who once published a translation of the Cairo part in *Die Liebespoesie der Alten Ägypter* (Leipzig, 1895), p. 43, rendered *idg* (in line 20) as "Kopftuch". He was a century later followed by Bernard Mathieu in *La poésie amoureuse de l'Égypte ancienne* (BdE 115, Le Caire, 1966), p. 100, who translated "foulard".[8] That is, most Egyptologists stick to the rendering "kerchief". Kemp and Vogelsang-Eastwood, however, in their recent study *The Textile Industry at Amarna* (London, 2001), p. 446, seem to follow Edel since they write that *idg* is "the lower wrap-around".

My main argument to reject Edel's interpretation is that *idg* appears to be the only word in our material that could indicate the kerchief. That a headcloth was regularly worn by the workmen and their families, living and working in the desert, cannot be doubted. Hence the item of dress must regularly turn up in the laundry lists. On the other hand, the "wrap-around" could be meant by *ifd*, or perhaps by *mrw*.

Notes

1) *JEA* 52 (1966), 85, note j. Repeated in *Commodity Prices*, p. 282.
2) *Pharaonic Egyptian Clothing*, p. 171.
3) Same work, p. 172 ff.
4) In *Hittite and Other Anatolian and Near Eastern Studies in Honour of Sedat Alp* (Ankara, 1992), pp. 127-135.
5) The numbers are the same when they are low (1 to 4), but see Edel's example 13: 6-3. See also his Ex. 6: 690-489; Ex. 7: 179-168; Ex. 15: 31-29; Ex. 18: 181-43 (!). Edel does not quote Pap. Harris I, 63b, 1-3: 428-399. Note that here the number of *idg* is higher.
6) Edel overlooked the case of Pap. Harris 63b (quoted above), where one *h3mn* – whatever that may be – also appears between *idg* and *mss*. Moreover, some of his examples are actually reconstructions (his nrs. 10 and 16); see also his p. 132.
7) Here vocalized as . The DeM part was not known until Posener published the fragments together in 1992.
8) In his note 367 Mathieu refers to my interpretation (see note 1 above). So does Grandet in his note 283 to the translation of Pap. Harris I (= BdE 119/II, Le Caire, 1999, p. 79).

pyr

The word *pyr* I have found in 13 instances in as many ostraca, and once in a Late Ramesside Letter (Pap. Bibl. Nat. 197, V, vs. 2 = Černý , *LRL*, p. 35).[1] Six of the occurrences are noted in lists of garments. Not a single price of it is recorded.

The Rameside letter tells us that some old and torn clothes (*ḥbs.w is m sfḫ*) should be made into "bandages to wrap up men with them" (*pyr r wt rmṯ im.w*). Does that mean that these strips of cloth were used for the treatment of the bodies of deceased persons?[2] Anyhow, their appearance in the lists suggests rather a function in everyday life. In O. DeM 242, 4 we read: [*py*]*r n ḏrww*, "of the flank" [3], which seems to imply that a body-strap was meant.

In O. DeM 187, 5 - vs. 1, the *pyr* is stated to be of *insy*, "red linen", and to measure 3 cubits and 3 palms by 5 palms in width, that is, about 180 by 22½ cm. That fits more or less the translation "strip", although almost 2 metres is fairly long.[4] In O. Turin 57366, vs. 2, "their *pyr*" are said to be *dg3 m nwb*, "covered in gold"; evidently a show-piece.

The data for the nature of *pyr* are rare. Even the spelling of the word is not without problems. It is conspicuous that it is never, so far as I know, written with . Obviously, it sounded differently. Usually we find  or ; once (a mistake ?) 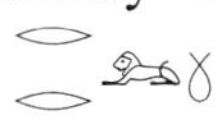 (O. DeM 87, 7).[5] Hannig's *Grosses Handwörterbuch*, p. 286, transcibes *pry* (with *y* at the end), and so do others. Why is not clear. It seems to me that there was a vowel between the *p* and the *r* which was important to indicate. A spelling *pry* (* 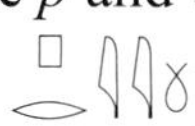) does not occur in our material.

One enigmatic instance is O. DeM 258, 4. Černý transcribed here, after a break, , but the  could easily be a  , as in line 5 ( for ). However, the present *pyr* is never written 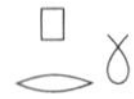; at least it appears as (in O. DeM 283, vs. 4), Yet, McDowell, *Village Life*, nr. 31 (p. 59) translates it as “bands”, so she too takes it to be our *pyr*.

In Pap. Anastasi IV, 3, 1 and in Pap. Koller 3, 2 what looks to be the same word is written , which strengthens the supposition that there was a sound between the *p* and the *r*. In both instances *pyr* is followed by *n pḥ.wy.f*. Caminos, *Late-Egyptian Miscellanies*, translates (p. 132 and p. 437): “He binds cloth-strips to its (?) end [for the purpose of wearing a *sḏy*-garment]”. What this means I fail to understand. It seems to me more likely that *pḥ.wy.f* means “his behind”, and that the strips were worn as a loincloth.

As for the spelling *ptyr* in these texts, Caminos suggests (p. 136), after Černý, that it is the same word as *pry* (so he writes it usually). That does also Meeks in his review of Hoch, *Semitic Words*, in *BiOr* LIV, 1997, 42, where he discuses writing *pdr* in Pap. d’Orliney , 6, which Hoch quotes on his p. 124. Hannig, *Grosses Handwörterbuch*, agrees with this, for he refers from *pdr* to *ptr*, and from that to *pry*.

Notes

1) According to the last reference to *Wb*. I, 531, 15 (*prj*), the word would also occur in Pap. Leiden I 352, 10, but that is a mistake. According to Černý (*JEA* 23, 1937, 186) the piece of textile in that line is *ḥpt*, “clew of yarn”.
2) See for this use: Philippe Collombert, “La bandelette-*pyr* au cou des deuillants” (*RdE* 57, 2006, 235-237).
3) It is not fully certain that indeed *pyr* was written, since only --  remains, but what else could it be?
4) In her study *Die Textilfärberei* (Äg. Abh., Bd 53, Wiesbaden, 1992), 127-128, Renate Germer quotes this entry and suggests this *pyr* – she writes *pj-ru* – is a piece of cloth and not a ready-made garment. On what grounds she bases this is not clear. In my opinion the occurrence of *pyr* in lists of garments shows that it was indeed a genuine item of dress; perhaps “garment” is not the correct term.
5) In Hannig’s, *Grosses Handwörterbuch*, p. 473, this is listed as *rrw* and translated “Band (zur Kleidung)”. That would mean that it is a different word (nowhere else written!). Or does it suggest that it is a variant of *mrw*? The use of the sign  (E 23) points rather to *pyr*.

The word *mrw*, when used for a piece of cloth, is mentioned 13 times in 11 ostraca, but, like *ỉsh*, never, so far as I am aware, in a Deir el-Medîna papyrus.

The word *mrw* can be written in two ways: as (with) and as , which is sometimes abbreviated to . There are also a few instances of , e.g. in O. Cairo 25572, 4 and O. DeM 211, 6. When spelled with it evidently indicates part of the human dress, while in the other spellings it usually means "bundle", of vegetables (*smw*) or papyrus (*w3ḏ*).[1] Yet, at least once *mrw* is written both with and : in O. Varille 19, II, 2. Here it clearly means an article of dress. In O. DeM 211, 6 – quoted above – it indicates that too, despite the writing, as the word *pḥw* ( ) which follows proves.[2]

The word *mrw* in all these spellings is derived from the verb *mr*, "to bind". Whether one takes it in its meaning "bundle" to be a different word from that of an item of dress is, I think, a matter of definition,[3] depending mainly on whether one takes the translation as a point of departure or not.

Here we are mainly concerned with the item of dress. This is in the ostraca three times said to consist of *nꜥꜥ* and once of *šmꜥ* (O. Petrie 42 = *Hier. Ostr.* 28/4, 5). Five prices of it are known, each of a single item, costing 5 deben or slightly more; cf. *Commodity Prices*, 287, Table XLVII.

The main problem is: what exactly is a *mrw*, and hence, how should it be translated? In *Commodity Prices*, 286-287, I first rendered it as "cloth strips", which would perhaps fit its occurrence in O. Cairo 25543, 13: *nꜥꜥ ḏ3y* 1 *m mrw*, "one cloak of smooth cloth with cloth strips". However, in another case it seems to be a more substantial object. In O. UCL 19614, 4

(Allam, *Hieratische Ostraka und Papyri*, 75) we read that a woman gave her husband one *mrw* (*iw.s ḥr dit n.i wꜥ mrw*) with the request to take it to the riverbank and sell it for one *sniw*.[4] When such an object could be sold on the market – note that it was called "one" (*wꜥ*) *mrw* – it can hardly have been a simple strip of cloth. McDowell, *Village Life*, 43 (nr. 18) translated it as "sash". In *Commodity Prices* I suggested that it may have been a similar piece of cloth as what elsewhere is called *pry* (i.e. *pyr*), but I am not sure that this was correct, whereas "sash" would well fit the older "strip of cloth".

Notes

1) E.g. O. Petrie 42 (= *Hier. Ostr.* 28/4), vs. 2, where *mrw* is written with 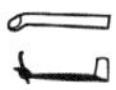 . What would be the difference between *mrw*, "bundle", and *ẖrst*, sometimes abbreviated to , I do not know.

2) Cf. *pyr n pḥ.wy.f* (above p. 30) and *sḏw ph.wy* (below, p. 46).

3) Hannig, *Grosses Handwörterbuch*, p. 347, presents the word for cloth-strip ("Binde, Zeugstreifen") and that for bundle in one entry, but does not note the spelling with  . Faulkner, *Concise Dictionary of Middle Egyptian*, p. 111, also mentions them as one word ("strip of cloth" and "bundle of clothes").

4) It was not sold, for the people on the market called it *bin*, "bad". Finally, the lady received no less than 1½ *khar* for it (vs. 3).

The word *mss* is one of the most common names for an item of dress, used by men and women. It occurs 112 times in 94 ostraca[1] and at least 12 times in 8 papyri from the Village. Until recently it was generally accepted that it indicated the "tunic". This was originally based on the meaning of the words *mss n ꜥḥꜣ*, "mail shirt" ("Panzerhemd"). To that Edel added the argument that *mss* indicated the same object as the Akkadian word *nahlaptu* (*SAK* 1, 1974, 118).[2] Moreover, the *mss* consisted mostly of the *nꜥꜥ* fabric. , also written 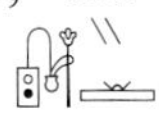(e.g. in O. Gardiner 123 = *Hier. Ostr.* 54/1, 6; O. Turin 57398, 1 and 57456, 5; O. Cairo 25590, 3 and 25602, 2), the heavier, coarser kind of cloth, which seems the most suitable for a tunic. Only seldom is the garment said to be made of *šmꜥ*, "thin linen" (O. Cairo 25677, 8; O. AG 140, 6), or, slightly more frequently, of *šmꜥ nfr*. "fine thin linen" (O. DeM 454, II, 4: O. Gardiner 233, 5; Pap. Cairo 65739, 13; Pap. Leiden I 352, 9).[3]

Once a writing of the word *mss* with  appears, namely in O. Glasgow D 1925.70 (= O. Colin Campbell 5 = *Hier. Ostr.* 63/1), I, 4. We read here: *dḥr*  *ir.n* 1 *oipě*, while in col. II, 1 is written: *wḥm di.t n.f ẖny dḥri mss* (). This is of course not the tunic but the "sack", usually written  (or with).

As stated above, everyone seems to agree that the correct translation of *mss* is "shirt, tunic".[4] For instance, Černý in *Hieratic Inscriptions from the Tomb of Tut'ankhamūn*, § 46, 5, or Wente in his *Letters*, nrs. 229 (O. DeM 125) and 249 (O. DeM 131). Admittedly, earlier, in his *Late Ramesside Letters* of 1967, p. 73, he translated Pap. Geneva D 191, vs. 18: *ḥbsw Pr-ꜥꜣ ꜥ.w.s m mss m šꜣiw* as "whom Pharaoh, l.p.h., has clothed with an apron as is fitting". And still a few years earlier, in

1961, I rendered *mss* in my dissertation *Two Ancient Egyptian Ship's Logs*, as it appears in Pap. Turin 2008 + 2016, II, 15 (p. 74), also as “apron”. But in *Commodity Prices*, 259-260, I too returned to the usual translation “tunic”. Already in 1911 Gardiner rendered it as “shirt” in Pap. Anastasi I, 25, 5 (*Egyptian Hieratic Texts*, Part I; reprinted in 1964); and in Pap. Chester Beatty I, vs. C3, 1 (of 1931) he wrote already “tunic”. Fischer-Elfert, *Die satirische Streitschrift des Papyrus Anastasi I* (= Ägypt. Abh. Bd 94, 1986, p. 213, note f) rendered *mss* as “Hemd”, but added “Tunika”. Finally, see Rosalind Hall, “The Pharaonic *mss* tunic () as a smock?” in *GM* 43 (1981), 29-38.

This general consensus was disturbed by Barry Kemp and Gillian Vogelsang-Eastwood in their *The Ancient Textile Industry at Amarna* (London, 2001), p. 442-443.[5] They raised serious doubts on the correctness of the translation. Their argument is that almost always the price of a *mss* is 5 *deben* (a few times 4 *deben*, but never more or less), while a loincloth costs 15 to 20 *deben*. Yet, a loincloth takes 1 metre of cloth, a tunic 2½ to 4 metres. Out of one tunic 3 loincloths could easily be made. If a tunic was so cheap, why did one not do so? A second argument is, that the size of the known tunics varies considerably, whereas the price is surprisingly stable.

All this is obviously correct. What we still miss is a suggestion as to what else a *mss* could be. Should we go back to “apron”? I doubt it. Whatever, this matter once more shows how limited our knowledge of the common Egyptian words for clothes still remains.

A few more details. In O. Nash 3 (= O. BM 65935 = *Hier. Ostr.* 56/2), 3, the *mss* is called *n ḳn*, “in perfect condition”; in O. Berlin P 12649, 2 only *ḳn*. On the other hand, in O. BM 29555, vs. 11, we find: *isy* () *n mss* 1, “one old (worn out) tunic”. In two texts the *mss* is called “large” (ꜥꜣ: O. AG

140, 4 and O. AG 142, 5 and 6), while in the latter text *ꜥꜣ* is both times followed by *šri*, "small". Finally, there is in our material one more extensive description, namely in Pap. BM 10068, II, 13: *mkw* () *m sfḫ mss* 2, "two tunics of tapestry woven fabric, being worn out". Moreover, a *mss* is called *n Pr-ꜥꜣ ꜥw.s* in O. Gardiner 103 (= *Hier. Ostr.* 52/2), vs. A, 9 and in O. DeM 931 (= O. AG 25), 3.

As regards the gender of the word, we find a few times a *t* added to *mss*, e.g. in O. Gardiner 123 (= *Hier. Ostr.* 54/1), 6; O. DeM 283, 4; O. IFAO 1055, 1a and 7 (both times , with one  !). This is exceptional, although the word was probably indeed feminine. That is shown by the use of *tꜣ* or *tꜣy* before it: O. Petrie 67 (= *Hier. Ostr.* 20/1), 4; O. DeM 580, 6 (twice); O. Cairo 25721, 9. In his *Grosses Handwörterbuch*, p. 364, Hannig lists *mss* and *msst* as two different words, although both translated as "Tunika, Ghalabiya". That looks to me over-correct. It is simply a matter of a more or less accurate spelling. Perhaps in the daily vernacular the *t* was mostly dropped.

Notes

1) In O. BM 50711, 2 the publication has 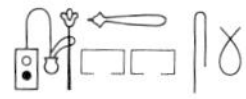 for what certainly is ; see the photograph. Cf. above, Chapter 2, note 31 end.
2) Repeated in his article on *idg* in the *Studies in Honour of Sedat Alp*; see above, p. 19, note 4.
3) Here written *šmᶜ nfr*  (see *JEA* 23, 1937, 18b); for , see above, p. 23.
4) I prefer "tunic" above "shirt" ("Hemd"), since that may give the impression that the garment covers only the upper part of the body.
5) In her *Pharaonic Egyptian Clothing* (1993), p. 130, note 1, Dr. Vogelsang-Eastwood still sticks to the interpretation of *mss* as "bag-tunic". She rejects my "translation" with *ghalabiyah*. That is certainly correct insofar as a *ghalabiyah* is of a different shape. What I argued (*Commodity Prices*, 260) was only that the *mss* played the same rôle in daily life.

rwḏw

In 52 ostraca I found this word 72 times, as well as 38 times in 14 papyri from Deir el-Medîna (16 of these 38 times in Pap. BM 10068, vs. I). That is more than most other items of dress. Clearly *rwḏw* formed part of the everyday attire of the workmen.

There is a word *rwḏw* which means “firm, steady”, and suchlike, but a relation between it and the present word is not at all clear. There is more chance that there was a connection with *rwḏ*, “bowstring”, the more so since the present word is usually, apart from a phonetic complement , written with sign T 12 ( ).[1] In a few instances the *ḏ* is omitted, so that we find only . That is for instance the case in O. DeM 937, 2, but here Grandet transcribed *d(ꜣj)w*. Exactly the same form occurs in O. DeM 10021, 4, but here *dꜣỉw* precedes, so that the reading *rw*[*ḏw*] is certain, also to Grandet. Generally, I think that the presence of the sign is decisive, but there seems to be one exception. In O. DeM 943, 3 Grandet transcribes (with a *d* !). The text runs: *ỉw pꜣy dw* (!) 2 *r pḥ.t.f*. The addition *r pḥ.t*[*y*].*f* seems to show that indeed *dꜣỉw* is meant.

There are some instances where the word *rwḏw* is written only as : O. BM 5643 (= *Hier. Ostr.* 85/2), 8; O. DeM 258, 7; O. Cairo 25684, 4. In O. DeM 452, 4 occurs even alone, without . Since it is a list of garments, it is evidently the present word.

In my *Commodity Prices*, p. 284-285, I discussed what *rwḏw* as an item of dress could be, reaching the conclusion, although with hesitation, that the translation could be “shawl”.[2] It is important to note that a *rwḏw* is more than once said to be part of the dress of a woman.[3]

Valbelle, *Les Ouvriers*, p. 282, draws attention to the fairly common combination of *mss* and *rwḏw*, arguing that the latter can hardly be anything else than the piece of cloth knotted around the loins, over the tunic. As for a convincing picture she refers to the paintings in the tomb of Anherkhew the Younger (TT 359).[4] On account of this evidence she calls the *rwḏw* an "apron" ("pagne"). I am not convinced that this is the correct term and would prefer the word used by Gillian Vogelsang-Eastwood: "sash-kilt".[5] As stated before, the problem is that our modern terminology does not fit the ancient Egyptian reality.[6]

The measurements of a *rwḏw* are recorded in Pap. BM 10052, II, 25 (Peet, *Tomb Robberies*, pl. XXXVI). They are: 8 by 4 cubits, about 4 by 2 metres. The word "bowstring" would suggest a less wide length of cloth. Perhaps the suggestion "shawl" was not too far from the truth, though "sash" would have been clearer. What, however, is then the difference between *rwḏw* and *mrw*?

The *rwḏw* is mostly said to consist of *nʿʿ*; less frequently of *šmʿ*, as for instance in O. DeM 454, vs. I, 2 (in rt. II, 7: *nʿʿ*) and in O. Turin 57150, 5. In the papyri it occurs four times with *šmʿ*, and twice with *šmʿ nfr*: Pap. BM 10052, II, 25 (quoted above) and Giornale dell'anno 17 B, vs. 9, 2. But in the papyri too *nʿʿ* occurs often.

Twice a *rwḏw* is called *n ḳn*, "in perfect condition": in O. AG 142, 7 and in Pap. Chester Beatty III, vs. 5, 2, while also twice it is called *thȝ*, "damaged": in O. Berlin P 12649, 3-4 and Pap. Turin 1885, vs. II, 6. Only once it is called *šri*, "small": in O. IFAO 1055, 4, where two others precede which were obviously of a normal size. All this, in itself not important, shows that every condition noted for other garments turns up at least once for a *rwḏw*.

Notes

1) There are a few exceptions: O. DeM 583, II, 3; O. Gardiner 223, 1, 2 and 3; O. Berlin P 9408, 2, 3 and vs. 13 (all these ; in vs. 6 and vs. 12 , but nowhere ); O. Brussels E 304, 4 and 5 ( only).
2) That is also the translation of Peden in Pap. Mallet I, 13 and II, 1 (but not in I, 9 !); see his book *The Reign of Ramesses IV*, p. 117. Grandet translates "chale roudou", which shows that he thought it to be a particular type of shawl.
3) The *rwḏw* of Weight 5165 is also of a woman: cf. Valbelle, *Catalogue des Poids*, p. 21. In his translation of Pap. Harris I (vol. 2, note 357) Grandet calls the *rwḏw* "une pièce de l'habillement féminine, peut-être un chale",
4) See e.g. W. Vivian Davies (ed.). *Colour and Painting in Ancient Egypt* (London, 2001), pl. 27.
5) *Pharaonic Egyptian Clothing*, p. 64 ff. Some examples from Deir el-Medîna tombs are: from the tomb of Nebenmaat (TT 219) = Maystre, *La tombe de Nebenmât* (Le Caire, 1930), pl. VII, 4 (scene 53); from the tomb of Neferabu (TT 5) = Vandier, *La tombe de Nefer-Abou* (Le Caire, 1935), pl. X bottom (first figure before Anubis); from the tomb of Kha'bekhent (TT 2) = Bruyère, *Tombes thébaines de Deir el Médineh à décoration monochrome* (Le Caire, 1952); pl. III (top left); etc.
6) Slightly disturbing is perhaps the occurrence of the word *rwḏw* (written ; the determinative is unclear), which is directly followed by *rd.wy twt*, "sandals", in O. Anthes II, 4 (unpublished). In line 5

it seems to be noted that its value was 2 *khar*, somewhat less than that of the sandals in I, 4, which cost for a pair 3 *khar*. Hence one could suggest that in I, 4 the *rwḏw* was connected with sandals, but it can hardly mean "shoestring".

ẖnk

This name of an item of dress I have found 35 times in 28 ostraca, but not once in a Deir el-Medîna papyrus. It is exceptional in the way that no price of it is known, the reason why it was not discussed in my *Commodity Prices*. It occurs only once in a list of clothes in Pap. Harris I, namely in 63a, 9, and only once its material () is noted, namely in O. Berlin P 12649, 3.[1] In the ostraca, however, it is not rare!

The word *ẖnk* occurs a few times in papyri not from the Village, e.g. in Pap. Sallier IV, vs. 15, 4, or in the Middle Kingdom "Story of the Sporting King", 3, 2 (); cf. Caminos, *Literary Fragments in the Hieratic Script*, pl. X and p. 31. Yet, nowhere in the dictionaries or elsewhere does there seem to be any suggestion as to its shape or function.[2]

An exception is Wente's translation (*Letters*, nr. 194) of *ẖnk* in O. Gardiner 67 (= *Hier. Ostr.* 47/2), 4, for which he suggests hesitatingly "undergarment". In O. DeM 626, 2 (*Letters*, nr. 253) he even dares to be more specific, translating "underpants(?)". This was followed by Andrea McDowell, *Village Life*, nr. 31 (p. 59), when she translated *ẖnkỉꜣ* in O. DeM 258, 3 and 7 as "underpants", without Wente's question mark. On what grounds this rendering was based is, so far as I know, never explained.

In. O. Gardiner 67, just quoted, the *ẖnk* is said to be "of 6 cubits", i.e. over 3 metres; a width is not mentioned. It is also said to be "not with holes" (*ỉw bn sw thꜣm*). In O. IFAO 385, 2 (unpublished: Černý's Notebook 104) we read: *ỉẖ dỉ.k wꜥ ẖn*[*k*] *r pḥ.wy, pꜣ-wn nn wn r pḥ.wy*; "Please, give you [me] a *ẖnk* to [my] behind, for there isn't one on [my] behind". Whatever the interpretation of this letter, by a certain Kha'y to his father – which is not very clear – it appears that a *ẖnk* was, or could be, worn on the behind, like the *sḏw / sḏy*.[3] That is also clear from

O. Nash 6 (= O. BM 65936 = *Hier. Ostr.* 56/1, 10-11: *ỉw bw ỉr.t.s n.ỉ ẖ*[*n*]*k r pḥt.ỉ*, "she has not made me a *ẖnk* for my behind.[4]

The problem is: what distinguished the *ẖnk* from other garments (kilt, loincloth, apron) worn on the lower part of the body? Wente hesitated to translate "underpants". There are indeed representations in which a man seems to wear more than one kilt. Was indeed a special word used for a garment shaped like another (a kilt or a loincloth) because it was worn under it? Or is it rather what Gillian Vogelsang-Eastwood, *Pharaonic Egyptian Clothing*, p. 65, calls a "sash-kilt"? This is something between a sash and a kilt. The length of 3 metres would perhaps suit it.

By far the majority of the occurrences of *ẖnk* are found in lists of clothes, although not all. Since some of these lists explicitly record laundry (e.g. O. DeM 258 and O. Gardiner 193) it is evident that the garment belonged to the normal everyday life of the workmen.

As regards the spelling of the word, in some instances, as in O. Nash 6 mentioned above, the *n* of *ẖnk* is omitted. It does also incidentally end in  (e.g. in O. DeM 212, I, 1, 5 and 9) or in [5] (e.g. in O. DeM 258, 3 and 7), while in still other instances a second *n* appears (e.g. in O. DeM 211, 3: ). Twice we find even 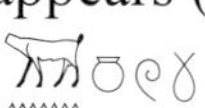(O. DeM 769, 9 and 924, 4), and once, in O. IFAO 1055, 3, *ẖnkt* (with a *t*), although the word is certainly masculine.[6] Allam's transcription of O. Brussels E 6311, vs. 10 (Allam, *Hieratische Ostraka und Papyri*, 27) has , but the  looks doubtful (see the photograph on p. 26). It seems here to be followed by *ꜥ3*, "large", as in O. Gardiner 210, 1.[7]

All these details are not surprising. The only real problem is: what garment was called *ẖnk*? Was it indeed "underpants"?

Finally, this *ẖnk* should be distinguished from *ẖnw* / *ẖnt*, “hide, skin”,[8] which in some cases is almost identically written, and appears also as an item of dress. In O. DeM 769, 9, for instance, in a list of garments, we find . Grandet translated it as “peaux”, as also in O. DeM 924, 4; that is, he neglects the information of the determinative. As I stated above, I would rather think that the sign  (and not 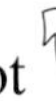!) definitely points to a garment of cloth. Moreover, these texts are lists of textiles. The omission of the *k* may be misleading, but is not essential, no more so than the omission of the *n* in O. Nash 6 (discussed above).

That our *ẖnk* is the same word as 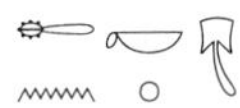 in *Coffin Texts* IV, 183i, as Faulkner, *The Ancient Egyptian Coffin Texts*, vol. I, p. 260, note 32 (“doubtless”) states (he writes *ẖn-kt*), seems to me no more than a vague possibility. Anyhow, the determinative shows that it was there not made of cloth.

Notes

1) Černý (Notebook 104) noted after this *nꜥꜥ* only a facsimile. But  seems to me rather clear.
2) Grandet, for instance, states in his note 849 to Pap. Harris I: "un vêtement non identifié mais souvent mentionné".
3) Cf. O. Černý 3 + O. Fitzwilliam Museum (K*RI* VII, 190), 1, 7: *ḫr nn*  *r ph.ty*. For *sḏy*, see below.
4) In her *Village Life*, p. 46, McDowell translates: "a garment for my behind", without any suggestion as to what kind of garment; in contrast to her translation of O. DeM 258 (see above).
5) See above, p. 16.
6) In O. Vienna H 3 (= *Hier. Ostr.* 45/3), vs, 3, for instance: *pꜣy.f ẖnk*; in O. DeM 626, 2: *pꜣ*.
7) Černý transcribed (Notebook 31, p. 17): ; what else than *ẖnk* could this be?
8) E.g. O. Petrie 37 (= *Hier. Ostr.* 29/3), 4 (); O. DeM 321, 2 (); O. Petrie 48 (= *Hier. Ostr.* 31/4), 8 ( *nt ꜥnḫ*).

sḏw / sḏy

This word occurs over 110 times in about 80 ostraca, and 11 times in 10 Deir el-Medîna papyri. At least, if indeed the three ways in which it is supposed to have been written, with , and , all indicate the same object.[1] That and are variants is rather certain. In some instances it is even difficult to see in the hieratic text which of the two signs, or , is meant. Whether the words with are also mere variants is less obvious.[2] In O. DeM 198, for instance, and occur directly after each other (lines 1 and 2 of col. I);[3] in O. DeM 404, 1, *ḏ3y* is followed by , while in line 2 *rwḏw* precedes . But most disturbing is O. DeM 925,[4] 5: *p3* *hn*ʿ *p3* [ ]. Grandet, in his publication of this text,[5] suggests that the last word (he reads it as "sédjouy") has a continuation, which is lost, either *n pḥ.wy, n ḥ3t*, or *n ḏrt*. Against that I could remark that is indeed known in the phrase *s3ḏw n ḏrt* (O. DeM 86, 7 and 452, 7),[6] but *sḏw n pḥ.wy* appears only with (O. DeM 87, 2 and 583 II, 1) or (O. DeM 452, 8 and O. Cairo 25612, 4).[7] The phrase *n ḥ3t* I do not know from any ostracon, only from Gurob Fragment U, C3 (*RAD* 23, 9), but then one should also mention *sḏw ḥr* and *sḏw n ḳdt* (both) from O. Brunner, 2 (*ZÄS* 111, 1984, 7 and K*RI* VII, 249). That is, the only likely addition to [ ] in O. DeM 928, 5 seems to be *n ḏrt*; or perhaps *s3ḏw n* .

Even if this would be correct, there are still the two cases O. DeM 198 and 404. I do not see a solution for the problem. If the former with  would indeed be another word, that is, indicate another garment, I do not know whatever it could be.

In order to complicate the matter even more, there occurs in a few ostraca a word , viz. in O. DeM 90, 7 and 211, 5[8] in the phrase *sd n ḏrt*, and in O. DeM 30, 7 as *sd šrỉ n pḥ.wy*. The suggestion that this *sd* is a variant of *sḏw* / *sḏy* is strengthened by the occurrence of  *ph.wy* in O. Cairo 25612, 4 and O. DeM 452, 8,[9] and by  *n ḏrt* mentioned above.

A word *sd* is well known in the meaning "tail".[10] The word *sd* with the determinative of garment indeed always contains also a tail-hieroglyph, but this is never used in the three variants of *sḏw* / *sḏy*. Yet, all four seem to indicate the same object, usually thought to be a "loincloth". Indeed, there could be a connection with "tail" if it is a triangular piece of cloth worn between the legs. Yet, if the word throughout indicates the loincloth, why then the phrase *sḏw n pḥ.wy*? And what could be a *sḏw n ḏrt*: "loincloth of the hand"?? Or a *sḏw ḥr* and *sḏw n ḳdt*, as in O. Brunner? Evidently, when used in such expressions, *sd* or *sḏw* / *sḏy* means simply "cloth"; while used alone the latter means specifically "loin-cloth".

Valbelle (*Les Ouvriers*, p. 283, note 3) remarks that the prices of *sḏw* / *sḏy* seem too high for a simple loincloth ("petit triangle de tissu"), Indeed, some are unbelievably high (see *Commodity Prices*, Table XLIII on p. 275); one even perhaps 30 *deben*, and that is also the value in O. Turin 57061, 3 which had not yet been published when I wrote that book. In some instances one could explain it since the material is stated to be *šmꜥ nfr*, but the *sḏy* in the Turin ostracon consisted perhaps of *nʿʿ*. The difference in price with a *mss*, which almost always cost 5 *deben* is striking.

On the other hand, in Pap. Anastasi IV, 3, 1, as well as in the parallel text, Pap. Koller 3, 2, we read: "He binds cloth-strips (*ptyr* = *pyr*) to his behind for the purpose of wearing (*ṯꜣy*) a *sḏy*". And in O. Černý 19 (= *Hier. Ostr.* 54/4), vs. 2-5, the addressee of this letter is told "to take this rag of a kilt and this rag of a *sḏỉꜣ* (*pꜣy ỉsw n sḏỉꜣ*[11]) to make the kilt into red linen cloth (*ỉnsy*) and the *sḏỉꜣ* into an apron (*šndt*).[12] That seems to suggest that the *sḏy* was not really small. Finally, we find rather frequently in lists of garments that *dꜣỉw* / *dw* is directly followed by *sḏw* / *sḏy*, which could mean that they formed a set: a kilt plus a loincloth.[13]

Our word "loincloth" may call up the notion of underwear, but that would be wrong. In the *Wisdom of Amenope*, XXI, 1 (Chapter 20) we read: *m dit ḥr.k m sḏw wbẖt*, which Miriam Lichtheim (*Ancient Egyptian Literature*, vol. II, p. 158) renders: "Do not incline to the well-dressed man". Somewhat more literal, Irene Grumlach in her *Untersuchungen zur Lebenslehre des Amenope* (*MÄS* 23, 1972), p. 134, translated: "Wende dich nicht dem Leuchtenden Gewande zu". Admittedly, this text is centuries younger than our ostraca, but it is clear that *sḏw*, if it is here a substantive, cannot be a word for underwear.

Summarizing: although I very well see the objections against the usual translation "loincloth" for all four variants, I fail to see another solution. McDowell, in her *Village Life*, also keeps it; except in O. DeM 30, 7 (her nr. 32, on p. 60), where she translates 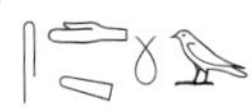 *n ph.wy* as "sanitary towel". This is probably on account of the word *šrỉ*. In the same text, line 6, she renders , as usual, with "loincloth".[14]

Finally, it may be useful to point out some doubtful cases. In O. DeM 90, 5 and 6. Černý transcribed . I am convinced that was meant.[15] In line 5 the garment is called *ḳn*, “in perfect condition”; in the next line *ỉs*, “old, worn out” (only is written!). *n ḳn* is also noted in Pap. Vienna 34, 2 (K*RI* VII, 173), while in line 5 of that text the four *sḏw* are said to be *thꜣ*, “damaged”. The word *ỉsw* occurs, except in O. DeM 90, 6, also in O. DeM 210, III, 7 (again only), in O. DeM 554, vs. 3-4;[16] in O. Černý 19 (= *Hier. Ostr.* 54/4), vs.3–4 (*pꜣy* *n sḏỉꜣ*), and in O. Varille 19, I, 4 (*sꜣḏwy*). The garment is also said to be *thꜣ* in O. Glasgow D. 1925.78 (= O. Colin Campbell 13), 3, while in O. BM 50737.5 a *sḏy* is called *šꜥd* ( ), “torn, mutilated”.

Once a *sḏw* is stated to be n *Pr-ꜥꜣ ꜥ.w.s*: in O. DeM 929, 4. Finally, intriguing is the addition *n kdt* ( ) in O. Brunner, 2 and 5, mentioned above.[17]

Notes

1) So already Gardiner, *Hieratic Papyri in the British Museum.Third Series: Chester Beatty Gift*, vol. I (Text), p. 25, note 13 (note to Pap. Chester Beatty III, vs. 5, 2).
2) The problem has already been discussed in *Commodity Prices*, p. 272-273.
3) Andrea McDowell, *Village Life*, nr. 48 (p. 69) translates both as "loincloth", which looks not very convincing.
4) Mentioned in *Commodity Prices*, p. 273, as O. IFAO 362, since it was then not yet published.
5) *Catalogue des ostraca hiératiques non littéraires*, Tome IX, p. 101.
6) Note that there occurs also twice  *n ḏrt*: O. DeM 90, 7 and 211, 5. For that *sd*, see below.
7) In O. Černý 3 + O. Fitzwilliam 1 (K*RI* VII, 190), 7: *ẖr nn wn*  *r pḥ.ty*. This expression "there is no garment to his behind" occurs in O. Nash 6 (= *Hier. Ostr.* 56/1), 10-11, and in O. IFAO 385, 2 (unpublished) with *ẖnk* (see above, p. 30, and in O. Turin 57093, vs. 5-6, with *ḥbsw*.
8) Possibly also in O. DeM 258,6, but here what follows  is lost. The sign , which also occurs in O. DeM 211, 5, is derived from *sḏ*, "to break".
9) Cf. also *mrw pḥ.wy* in O. DeM 211, 6, after *sd n ḏrt*. What nuance was expressed by this *mrw* I do not know.
10) In the *Wb. der mediz. Texte*, II, 823, it is noted that *sd* means also "tampon".

11) This ending - *ỉꜣ*, typical for all kinds of word for garments (see above, p. 16), occurs also in O. DeM 258 (four times) and O. DeM 10105,2.

12) Cf. Renate Germer, *Die Textilfärberei und die Verwendung gefärbter Textilien im Alten Ägypten* (Wiesbaden, 1992), p. 128.

13) Grandet translates *sḏw / sḏy* as "bande-culotte" (e.g. in O. DeM 865, 924, 925 and 929). In his translation of the Papyrus Harris I – where it occurs six time – he renders it "bande (?) *sḏw*"; cf. vol. 2, note 282 (note to 14a, 14). He explains it to be the triangular or roughly triangular piece of cloth one sees hanging in front of a *šnḏyt*.

14) In O. DeM 258, 6 she translates (her nr. 31 on p. 59)  as "[hand?] kerchief". Clearly supposing that *n ḏrt* has been lost (after O. DeM 90, 7 and 211, 5).

15) It would not be the only instance of an incorrect  ; cf. O. Berlin P 11259, 4: 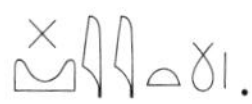.

16) Wente, *Letters*, nr. 245 (p. 160) translates "the shabby loincloth".

17) This O. Brunner appears to be the same text as the O. Hasany Abdel-Galil; cf. Hannig, *JEA* 90 (2004), 219; see K*RI* VII, 414-415.

The garment called *dꜣỉw*, abbreviated *dw*, occurs also about 110 times in 89 ostraca, plus 33 times in 21 papyri from Deir el-Medîna; that is more frequently than *mss* or any other word for an item of dress. In two instances where Grandet reads *dꜣjw*, O. DeM 937, 2 and 943, 3, I would prefer *rwḏw*; see above, p. 38.

Although the word is usually, for instance in dictionaries, written as *dꜣỉw*, it occurs several times as *dꜣỉꜣ*,[1] and in ostraca mostly as *dw*, which is also found in some papyri. The first sign ( ) is occasionally so badly shaped in hieratic that the accurate transcription would be *rw* ( ), or even, rarely, , e.g. in O. Nims (= *Hier. Ostr.* 62/1), 5 and in O. Gardiner 133, 9 and vs. 2 (K*RI* VII, 182). A not uncommon determinative group is ,[2] which also can stand alone for *dꜣỉw*, e.g. in O. DeM 452, 2.[3]

The writing of *dꜣỉw* has for a long time been problematic; see Dévaud's article on the word in *ZÄS* 49 (1911), 106-116. Many times in the Old and Middle Kingdom hieratic texts it appears as one sign plus a determinative (S28). That sign, or , could be read as or as , but also as . Therefore one could hesitate whether what looks like or or is actually a deformation of ,[4] which Gardiner called "a garment", but which Henry Fischer (*MMJ* 10, 1975) argued to represent "a folded length of cloth". That looks indeed to be correct.

Generally, *dꜣỉw* has been translated as "kilt", or, when worn by a woman, as "skirt".[5] So for instance by Wente in his translation of the letters (e.g. in O. DeM 587, 6 = his nr. 219, or in O. Petrie 82 = his nr. 240) and by McDowell in her *Village Life* (e.g. in O. DeM 30, 5 = her nr. 32, or in O. DeM 258 = her nr. 31). Caminos, however, in his *Late Egyptian Miscellanies*, renders *d3ìw* with “loincloth”; e.g. in Pap. Bologna 1094, 1, 1, on his p. 3, or in Pap. Anastasi V, 13.4, on his p. 242. Since “loincloth” is, I think, the translation of *sḏw* / *sḏy* this cannot be correct.

Quite a different, and slightly disturbing, suggestion is that by Černý in his *Hieratic Inscriptions from the Tomb of Tut‘ankhamūn*, p. 11, namely “shawl”. I fail to see why he chooses this word. It seems to me that we have to stick to the translation “kilt”. That would suit the phrase in Pap. Harris I (14a, 10; 14b, 8; 63a, 4; 65a, 5): *d3ìw ḥry*, “overskirt”, or suchlike. The shape of the kilt, with its extensive pleating, may explain its rather high price, between 15 and 25 *deben* (see *Commodity Prices*, p. 266, Table XLII), higher than that of any other garment, except the *ḏ3yt*.

In a few lists the garment is said to be *ḳn* or *n ḳn*, “in perfect condition”: in O. DeM 90, 4, in O. Gardiner 219, 8, in O. AG 142, 10, and in Pap. Leiden I 352, 7. Twice this is contrasted to *ìsw*, “old”: in O. DeM 90, 3 and O. Gardiner 219, 8. That word *ìsw* turns also up in O. Varille 19, I, 5 (fully written  6) and in O. Černý 19 (= *Hier. Ostr.* 54/4), vs. 3-4 (“made into *ìnsy*”[9]). At least twice the *d3ìw* is said to be *thm* / *th3*, “damaged: in O. DeM 923, 3 and in Pap. Turin 1885, vs. II, 5 (K*RI* VI, 371); perhaps also in O. Gardiner 259, 2 ().

Once the *d3ìw* is stated to be *n Pr-ʿ3 ʿ.w.s.*: in O. Gardiner 265, 4,[10] while once the author of a text tells us that he received such a garment from Pharaoh: O. Petrie 18 (= *Hier. Ostr.* 70/1), 5. Also once a *d3ìw* is called *sẖt*, whatever that may mean.[11] A few times the wearing of a *d3ìw* is recorded, e.g. in O. DeM 49, 3 and 428, vs. 1, while in one ostracon we find that two of them were *nbd*, “plaited”: O. DeM 131, vs. 1 (written *ndb*!).

A few details may be of some interest. In O. Gardiner 133, 9 (K*RI* VII, 182) a *d3ìw* (written !) is called *n* *w3ḥ* *m ḏrw*; probably of some importance, but I fail to understand what it means. One can only hope once to find a parallel text. In Pap. Turin 2049/141[+], III, 5 (K*RI* VI, 635) a *dw* is followed by the words *sš ḥr.f* plus a price (the figure is lost). Here  seems indeed to mean *sš* and not *nꜥꜥ*, but what "written upon" a garment means is not clear. Or does *sš* here mean "painted"? That would explain what we read in O. DeM 49, 1: *pꜣ dꜣỉw sš.f*, "the kilt he painted".[12] Finally, it may be useful to note that *dꜣỉw ḥry*, "overskirt", which occurs several times in Pap. Harris I, does not once turn up in our present material.

Notes

1) See above p. 16. *dꜣỉꜣ* is found, e.g., in O. DeM 10098, 2; O. Gardiner 8 (= *Hier. Ostr.* 31/5), 1; O. Petrie 82 (= *Hier. Ostr.* 35/2), 4; O. Černý 19 (= *Hier. Ostr.* 54/4), vs. 3 and 4, and in several more ostraca, but not in the papyri.
2) In O. Ashmolean Museum 1945.37 + .33 (= *Hier. Ostr.* 74), 3 written ; in O. Cairo JdE 72474, b1: . The -sign is derived from , *tꜣ*.
3) See also Černý, *Hieratic Inscriptions from the Tomb of Tut'ankhamūn*, 51: *nty ỉm.f*: *ḏꜣy* 17, *ỉr. n*  34.
4) A sign between S26 and S27 in Gardiner's list, numbered N18, but clearly not meaning the same as that sign normally: "sandy tract".
5) Cf. e.g. O. Cairo 25725, 1-2: *ỉr ỉnk, dỉw wꜥ dꜣỉw n tꜣy.ỉ šrỉ*, "As for me, one skirt was given to my daughter". Also O. BM 29550, vs. 4: *dꜣỉw n st*, "a skirt of a woman". In Pap. Chester Beatty III, 9, 3, the garment is called *dw ꜥꜣmw*, "of the Asiatics". Whether in our language we would in this case call it a "skirt" and not a "kilt" is an open question.

6) In an ostracon found in the Valley of the Queens (Koenig, *BIFAO* 88, 1988, p. 124: Doc. XI, vs. 3) we find even 40 *dw* of *šmʿ nfr*.

7) The full writing  occurs also in O. BM 5633 (= *Hier. Ostr.* 86/1), vs. II, 1; O. DeM 113, 8; O. Gardiner 265, 4. In the "Lady Franklyn Hieratic Inscription" (K*RI* VII, 341-342), 3 it is written [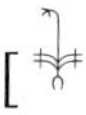]  .

8) The only time so far as I know that *ẖt* is said of a garment. For *ẖt* or *ẖt.tỉ* as used with baskets, see *Commodity Prices*, 140.

9) For *ỉnsy*, cf. Renate Germer, *Die Textilfärberei und die Verwendung gefärbter Textilien im Alten Ägypten* (Wiesbaden, 1992), 126 ff. For O. Černý 19, see there, p. 128.

10) In this list of clothes *rwḏw* (rt. 2) is also said to be *n Pr-ʿ3 ʿ.w.s.*, but not so the two *sḏw* or the *ỉsh* of line 3.

11) O. DeM 183, 3. The value of this *d3ỉ3* (sic) is by exception expressed in *khar*, and is low (2 *khar*); cf. *Commodity Prices*, 269.

12) For *ỉ.sš.f.* In *Commodity Prices*, 268, I expressed my doubts whether the painting of garments was ever mentioned, but see now Germer, *Die Textilfärberei*, 133.

ḏꜣyt

The name of this garment seems to occur 34 times in 29 ostraca[1] and 14 times in 11 Deir el-Medîna papyri. Although the word is certainly feminine – cf. for instance O. DeM 185, 4 and O. Berlin P 12343, 4: *tꜣ ḏꜣy* – the *ṯ* is seldom written, an exception being O. Berlin P 11259, 2. In O. DM 452, 1 we meet the rare form .

When the word turns up in a list of garments, which is fairly seldom, it mostly appears at the head of the list.[2] That may mean that it was the most important, for the most expensive item of dress. Its prices vary from about 20 *deben* up to 50, perhaps even to 60 *deben*.[3]

That the *ḏꜣyt* is a "cloak" (French: "manteau") is generally accepted. The measurements of it recorded in Gurob Fragment U (*RAD* 23, 4) are: 28 cubits and 4 palms to 4 cubits, that is, about 15 by 2 metres. Such a length of cloth had to be wrapped several times around the body, which is indeed possible.[4]

Usually the *ḏꜣyt* was made of *nʿʿ*; only six times in our material it is said to consist of *šmʿ*, and three times, in papyri, of *šmʿ nfr*. Evidently the ordinary, stronger fabric was more suitable for this outer garment.

Once a *ḏꜣyt* is said to be *n ḳn* (Pap. Vienna 34, 3), and once it is *ỉs*, "old" (O. DeM 790, vs. 2). Also once it was *šʿd* (), "mutilated": Pap. Turin 2104/223, vs. II, 10. In this last case its value was only 5 *deben*, as against 30 or 20 *deben* in vs. II, 4 and 5.

There seems to be no details recorded which could inform us about the use of this "cloak".

Notes

1) A few of them are not quite certain: O. IFAO 1008, 1 (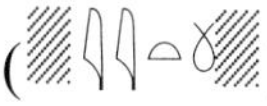), where the price, 25 *deben*, makes the interpretation likely, or O. DeM 790, vs. 2 (), probably "one old *ḏꜣy*". This garment is said to be mutilated (*šꜥd*); cf. Grandet, *Catalogue des ostraca hiératiques non littéraires*, Tome VIII, p. 62. Whether his translation of *m ḥr.f* is correct is uncertain.
2) An exception is O. AG 110 (now O. DeM 10067), where one *ḏꜣy* is listed after 1 *mss* and 5 *dꜣiw,* but before an *ỉfd*.
3) Cf. *Commodity Prices*, p. 279 (Table XLIV).
4) Cf. Gillian Vogelsang-Eastwood, *Pharaonic Egyptian Clothing*, 159 ff.

	Ostraca	Papyri	Together
ifd	47 (51)	6 (7)	53 (58)
ỉsh[1]	26 (32)	-	26 (32)
ỉdg	14 (18)	7 (9)	21 (27)
pyr	12 (12)	1 (1)	13 (13)
mrw	11 (13)	-	11 (13)
mss	94 (112)	8 (12)	102 (124)
rwḏw	52 (72)	14 (38[2])	66 (110)
ẖnk	28 (35)	-	28 (35)
sḏw / sḏy	78 (111)	10 (11)	88 (122)
dꜣỉw	89 (110)	20 (33)	109 (143)
ḏyꜣt	28 (33)	11 (14)	39 (47)
TOTAL	479 (599)	77 (125)	556 (724)

[1] eight times *ḥtri n ỉsh*
[2] sixteen of them in Pap. BM 10068, vs. I

TABLE I

The Number of Texts in which each Garment is mentioned
(between brackets the number of items)

	nʿʿ	*šmʿ*	*šmʿ nfr*	**Total**
ỉfd	28	1	2	31
ỉsh[1]	-	-	-	-
ỉdg	1	10	4	15
pyr	-	-	-	-
mrw	3	1	-	4
mss	53	2	3	58
rwḏw	38!	11	3	52
ẖnk	1	-	-	1
sḏw / sḏy	11	6	5	22
dꜣỉw	16	13	11	40
ḏyꜣt	16	6	1	23
Total	167	50	29	

Table II

The Frequency each type of Material is Noted

Chapter 4

Less Common Words for Garments

Beside the eleven words discussed in Chapter 3, each of which occurs more than ten times in our material from Deir el-Medîna – some even over a hundred – there are also some words for clothes in these texts which appear rarely. They are the subject of this chapter.

ꜥꜣt

In only two of our texts the word *ꜥꜣt* () occurs: in O. DeM 85, 3 and in O. DeM 769, 7,[1] both times at the end as a summary, preceded by 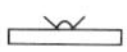 and followed by a figure. In the same function it is used in *Hieratic Inscriptions from the Tomb of Tut'ankhamūn*, §46, when Černý translates (p. 7) "choice linen".[2] The adjective "choice" seems to be due to the analogy with that other word *ꜥꜣt*, "costly/precious stone". I am not sure that it is here correct.

Our word *ꜥꜣt* is the ancestor of Demotic *ꜥꜣjw*, which is translated as "linen thread",[3] as well as of Coptic ϵιλλⲩ.[4] *ꜥꜣt* is used in medical and magical texts,[5] but it appears rarely elsewhere. In our ostraca it seems to mean "garments", but with some stress on the material, linen;[6] distinguished from the neutral word for garments *ḥbs*. As so many times, it is almost impossible to render it correctly by a single English word.

In a few other lists of clothes, e.g. O. DeM 404, 4 and O. Brussels E 304, 5, there is noted at the end  plus a figure, indicating the total of the garments. That may also be meant in O. DeM 867, although this is all, apart from the figure 9, that is written on the sherd. Whether in these cases  stands for *ꜥꜣt* is far from certain; it could as well be *ḥbsw*, as is written out in O. Gardiner 193, 6 (K*RI* VII, 311). In O. DeM 867 Grandet interprets as *ḥbs*, although with a query mark, referring to O. DeM 404, 4. I am not convinced that this is the only possibility.

ḥbs

Although out of the alphabetical order, this may be the place to discuss some instances of *ḥbs*. Once this word turns up in a list of garments between *pyr* and *sḏw*, namely in O. DeM 210, I, 5. Why in this case not the name of a specific garment is used is a mystery.

In the fragmentary O. IFAO 1021 (unpublished) we find, in line 4: … *s n Pr- ꜥꜣ ꜥ.w.s.* 1. This could mean: "one garment (*ḥbs*) of Pharaoh". Yet, *mss* is also a possibility. In O. Cairo 25572, 7 is noted: .[7] It could hardly be an abnormal way to write *ḥbsw sd*, "one *sd* / *sḏw* garment", the more so since the price 2 *oipě*, is far too low for that item of dress. What here is meant I fail to understand.

Finally, in O. DeM 404, where the summary is "ten garments" (see above), the last item before it is . That a specific piece of dress, a small one, is meant, is clear, for the number "one" is included in the total of 10. In O. DeM 865, 4 is written: , which Grandet transcribes as *ḏꜣy*(*t*) 1 and translates as "1 manteau". On what grounds he chooses this translation is not stated. These instances remain to me enigmatic.

ỉnt

The name of an item of dress, if indeed it was that, occurs six times in five ostraca, but so far as I know nowhere in a papyrus from the workmen's community. Five times it is written with ;[8] once, in O. Nash 16 (= O. BM 65934 = *Hieratic Ostraca* 41/3), vs. 3 as 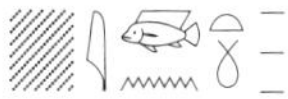.

The word has been connected with *nwt,* "yarn" (cf. e.g. Hannig, *Grosses Handwörterbuch Ägyptisch-Deutsch*, 76[9]), but is supposed to indicate a garment.[10] In O. Varille 13 (= O. Louvre E 27 678), 4 (K*RI* VII, 238) a coffin is said to be filled with *ỉnt*,[11] its value probably being 1 *snỉw*.

The other five instances do not occur in a context that explains anything about the nature of this garment. Hence its function in the sphere of dress remains as yet unknown.

bndw

This garment is mentioned in three ostraca: O. Cairo 25596, 2, O. DeM 579, 19, and O. Gardiner 210, 2 (unpublished). In the first one it is said to be of *nʿʿ*-cloth, in the others no such indication is noted. The word is throughout written with  (G29), but in O. Gardiner 210 this sign is almost completely lost; or was it a ? In O. Cairo 25596 the *n* is omitted.[12]

The word also occurs twice in Pap. Anastasi I (in 10, 3 and 28, 3[13]), both times as a verb, which Gardiner translated in the first instance (*bndw d̠rỉw*) as "(tightly) swathed", and the second as "wrapped up". We find the word also in Pap. Chester Beatty V, 8, 5 and VII, vs. 2, 1, the first instance in a list of all kinds of products. Gardiner translates here (p. 49) "gowns". The other case is most revealing: in a description of the goddess Anat we read that she was acting as a warrior, *sd.tỉ m ṯ3y.w, bndw.tỉ m ḥmwt*. Evidently, *sd*, "loincloth", is typical for men, *bndw* for women. Gardiner renders these words as "clad as men and girt as women".

It was perhaps this translation that led Hoch in his *Semitic Words in Egyptian Texts*, nr. 121[14], to render the verb as "to gird (clothes)", and hence the substantive *bndw* (nr. 122) as "probably belt". However, Meeks, in his review of Hoch's book (*BiOr* LIV, 1997, 40-41) argues, in my opinion correctly, that the verb means not "to gird" but "to wrap up", and that, therefore, the substantive *bndw* was a "pièce de tissu habituellement rectangulaire de taille variable"; that is, not a belt but a "wrap around dress".

Evidently, *bndw* is the name of a woman's garment, the only not too uncommon one for which no name has generally been accepted.[15] In my *Commodity Prices* I was still quite at a loss as to what it could be. Since then particularly Gillian Vogelsang-Eastwood, in her *Pharaonic Egyptian Clothing* (pp. 95-129) paid much attention to women's dresses, pointing out that there were three types: the wrap-around dress, the V-necked dress, and the bead-net dress. A name for the latter does, so far as I know, not occur in Deir el-Medîna texts, and whether the V-necked dress was still worn in this time is quite uncertain; this type dates, so far as preserved, from the Old and Middle Kingdoms. But the wrap-around dress was certainly worn by the women of the Village. The small number of instances in the texts may be an indication that it was not very common. Or does it mean that our evidence relates far more to men than to the women of the community?

Why the two prices of a *bndw* we have (*Commodity Prices*, 288-289), 1 *snỉw* and 2 *deben*, are so low is a problem, for a wrap-around cannot have been very small. But, as we have seen above (see *mss*, p. 35), the prices of clothes contain more such surprises. Was perhaps not the quantity of material but the shaping and sewing of the garments decisive for the price?

nfrw

Also in three ostraca a word *nfrw* is noted with the determinative  : in O. Gardiner 210, 5 (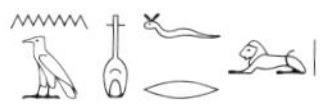 12 [16]), in O. IFAO 745, 1 () and in O. Turin 57464, 4 ( 2). Moreover, in O. DeM 1266 + O. Cairo 25218, 20, a love poem, there is a word [17], which looks to me the same.

Since our three instances all occur in lists of clothes there is no context that could throw light on the meaning of the word. It evidently indicated an item of dress, but was not very common.

In the Middle Kingdom *nfrw* was a term for garments of the gods (cf. *Wb.* II, 261). There was later even a title *ḥry ỉr nfrw n ỉmn*, "chief maker of *nfrw* of Amun"[18]. However, its appearance in three lists of human garments proves that not always a piece of dress of the deities was meant. Moreover, the mention of 12 *nfrw* in O. Gardiner 210 shows that it was not too rare. That in our texts "rags" was meant (see note 17) seems not very likely, but I fail to understand what garment it was.

ḥry-kꜥḥt

In four ostraca a piece of dress called *ḥry-kꜥḥt* is mentioned.[19] Since *kꜥḥt* means "shoulder" it is clearly a garment worn "over the shoulder", most probably a type of shawl.[20] Note that in O. DeM 255 no *t* is written. Perhaps also not in § 51a, 2 of the *Hieratic Inscriptions from the Tomb of Tutʿankhamūn*. In this publication, p. 11 note 1, Černý suggested also that it "might have been a shawl", but strangely enough he translated "sleeve". That, however, is most probably *ỉsḥ*; see above, p. 25.

In O. Černý 15 (= *Hier. Ostr.,* 61/3), vs. 17, the only text where the fabric is recorded, it is said to be *šmꜥ*. In the inscription from Tut'ankhamun's tomb quoted above it is mentioned among the garments (*ḥbsw*) consisting also of *šmꜥ*. This seems to well fit the meaning "shawl". However, what could be the difference between this object and the *rwḏw* (cf. above, p. 38-39), remains unclear. All we can state is that it was worn not around the neck but over the shoulder.

smꜣ

In only one laundry list, O. Gardiner 193 (K*RI* VII, 311),[21] there are recorded – at the end, line 5, just before the summary – two garments called *smꜣ* (). From Deir el-Medîna I know this word only from Pap. Mallet (= Pap. Louvre E 11006), II, 1 (K*RI* VI, 65), where it is said to consist of *nꜥꜥ* and is mentioned after *rwḏw*.

The word *smꜣ* also occurs in the *Hieratic Inscriptions from the Tomb of Tut'ankhamūn*, § 72, in a label with the words: *nty ỉm.s, smꜣ šri* 5,[22] as well as on the stela BM 588, 4 (*JEA* 49, 1963, 67, and 69 note g). Černý rendered it on the label of Tut'ankhamūn's tomb as: "1 small *smꜣ*", without any suggestion as to what garment was meant.

There is a verb *smꜣ*, "to join, to unite", but that does not help us, although our word may be derived from it. Nor is the expression *smꜣ-tꜣ*, "burial" helpful.

In Pap. Salt 124, I, 4, 6 and 8 this *smꜣ-tꜣ* is determined by  (cf. *JEA* 15 (1929), pl. 42), but it means here simply "burial".

Hannig's Grosses *Handwörterbuch Ägyptisch-Deutsch*, p. 703, mentions a word *smꜣ*, which it translates as "Beutel" (bag), but that can hardly be meant in our text. It also lists at the very end of that page a *smꜣw* which is interpreted as "e. Kleidungsstück". Evidently, what our *smꜣ* could be is still a mystery.

šndyt

Better known than almost all relatively rare words for items of dress, but in our material less often mentioned than the common ones, is *šndyt* – in the ostraca usually written as *šndt* (). I know it from seven instances in six ostraca.[23] In O. Anthes, II, 3 (unpublished) it is said to measure 1 cubit, which proves that it was not really large.[24]

The usual translation of *šndyt* is "apron" (French: "pagne"). My rendering "kilt" in *Commodity Prices*, 289, was a mistake,[25] for that is *dꜣỉw*. In O. Černý 19 (= *Hier. Ostr.* 54/4), vs. 5, we read that the rag of a loincloth (*sḏỉꜣ*) should be made into a *šndwt*,[26] which again suggests that the *šndyt* was a fairly small piece of cloth.

In Pap. Harris I the garment is mentioned five times, twice in large numbers. In 55b1 there are listed 2968 of them, in 41b3 even 10196. In the first instance there are recorded in the preceding lines (55a, 16 and 17) the same number 2968 of necklaces (*šby.w*) and amulets (*ḫtm.w*), while the excessive figure of 10196 also is given for *ḫtmw*, *šby.w* and *šꜣšꜣ.w* (also a kind of necklace) in 41a, 13-15. They seem to be sets.

In O. AG 116, 2 (K*RI* IV, 448),[28] a tiny fragment, we read: …. *mr* () *šndt m ḳnt*. What this means is a problem. Is *mr* here part of the title *ỉmy-r šndt*? Did such a title indeed exist, beside the well-known *ḫrp šndwt*?

According to Gillian Vogelsang-Eastwood the apron in this time "had taken on a more decorative nature and was worn in various combinations with kilts, sash-kilts and bag tunics".[29] That could be the explanation of its fairly rare appearance in our ostraca, as against the high numbers in Pap. Harris I. Such show-aprons will not have been part of the everyday dress of the workmen.

The material of which the *šndyt* was made is in our texts never recorded. In Pap. Harris I it is said to be *šmʿ* or *šmʿ nfr*.

ḳḏmr

Once, in a list of garments, O. IFAO 745, 2 (unpublished), there occurs a word *ḳmr*, written .[30] That will be the same piece of dress that is called *ḳḏmr* (with a *ḏ*) in Pap. Harris I, 63b, 12. These two seem to be the only places where it appears. The word thus leads to various problems.

Firstly, one would expect it to be borrowed from another language. Helck, *Die Beziehungen Ägyptens zu Vorderasien* (Wiesbaden, 1960), lists it (p. 572, nr. 244) among the "asiatische Fremdworte". However, Hoch did not include it in his *Semitic Words in Egyptian Texts*. Was it derived from Hittite, or from still another language?

Then, Grandet, *Le Papyrus Harris I*, vol. II, note 850 (*ḳḏmr* ou *ḳḏmʿr*!) gives no indication as to what it could mean; he notes merely: "un vêtement de type inconnu". The dictionaries of Hannig and Lesko render it as "tunic", on what grounds is not stated. Why should a foreign word have been used for a so common garment, normally called *mss*? Moreover, in O. IFAO 745 it is directly followed by this *mss*, while in Pap. Harris I, 63b, *mss* precedes.

Unfortunately, I can do no more than pointing out the problem; I am unable to propose any acceptable solution.

knt / krt

This may be a suitable place to draw attention to another obscure word for what could be an item of dress, namely *knt* or *krt.* It seems not to occur in any ostracon, but it is known from Pap. Mayer A, 4, 7 ( [31]) and Pap. BM 10068, vs. 1, 4 (). At least, if in these instances the same object is meant. In the first text eight of them are recorded, in the other only one, which is said to consist of *nʿʿ*. Peet's translation of the last occurrence, in his *The Great Tomb-Robberies*, p. 92, as "coloured cloth a whip-lash (??)" is not anymore acceptable.

The word may also occur in Pap. Anastasi IV, 17, 2, written . It is there said to consist of *ỉns*(*y*), "red cloth". This is indeed a description of whips (*ỉsbr*). Caminos (*LEM*, 201) translated it hesitantly as "straps", although admitting that this was a guess.

Hoch, *Semitic Words*, nr. 471, suggests that it is a "cloak". He lists some Semitic words with which it could be related, even Greek ones (χλαῖνα, χλανίς, χλαμύς), stating that they are all likely to be "ultimately related" and that they "constitute various reflexes of a common near-eastern *Kulturwort*". What kind of cloak, if indeed any, the Egyptian word(s?) indicate remains obscure.

Finally, some words for what are evidently items of dress appear only once in our material, usually without any indication in the context as to their meaning. They are here briefly mentioned for the sake of completeness.

psdw

In O. DeM 86, II, 5, a list of clothes, between *ẖnk* and *ỉsh*, there is noted what Černý transcribed as  2, which seems to mean: “two *psdw*”.[32] The signs at the beginning cannot stand for *dw*, also because that occurs a few lines higher, nor is it likely to be *rwḏw*, which is usually – admittedly, not always – written with  .

One could suggest that our word was derived from *psḏ*, “nine”, as *ỉfd* will be related to *fdw*, “four”, but even if this would be correct, what it would mean remains obscure. Other relations, e.g. with *psḏ*, “back”, are also possible. Whatever, the word seems to occur for an item of dress only here, and its meaning is quite unknown.

nṯr

In another list, O. DeM 452, we find in line 5:  (no  !). Could this be the later word for “mummy wrappings”? Anyhow, it seems to be unique in such a list of garments.

h3wmn* (?) and *nws

In yet another list of clothes, O. DeM 865, Grandet reads line 3 with hesitation as , and the next one as . For the first word he suggests (p. 43) the reading *h3w*, which could, he notes, be an abbreviation of *h3wmn*, the name of a garment which occurs in Pap. Harris I, 14a, 11 and 63b, 2. Here too, however, the reading is uncertain. It is written , which seems clear, but in the note 279 to his publication on this papyrus Grandet writes that *mn* is perhaps a misinterpretation by the scribe of , and that the word here too is actually *h3w*, as in the ostracon. What garment it indicates remains an open question.

The word *nws* in line 4 of the same ostracon is mentioned by Hannig in his *Grosses Handwörterbuch Ägyptisch-Deutsch*, p. 399, as meaning "e. Krone", but also "Kopftuch (der Frauen)",[33] and that could also be the opinion of Grandet, for he translates the word as "foulard *nous*". Hence, a particular type of kerchief.

ỉsw

For the good order I mention briefly this word too, although it can hardly be said to indicate a garment, for *ỉsw* means "rag". It occurs in O. DeM 452, 6, a list of clothes, recording eleven of it. The word is of course derived from *ỉs*, "old". As such it appears i.a. in O. Varille 19 (see below, p. 78). It was known already in Middle Egyptian; see e.g. the *Admonitions of Ipuwer*, 7, 11: "See, those who owned robes (*ḏ3y.w.t*) are in rags (*ỉsy.w.t*)".

Although the words mentioned above occur in ostraca, the objects they indicate can, apart from *ỉsw*, hardly have been part of the everyday life of the workmen and their families. For that they are too rare – unless, of course, these garments were also known under another name.

In books on actual Ancient Egyptian dress space is devoted to leather loincloths,[34] of which some items are preserved in museums.[35] The best known may be that of Maiherperi in the Boston Museum of Fine Arts (Nr. 03.1035).[36] A special name for such a garment seems nowhere in our studies to be recorded. The only possibility I am aware of is, that it was called *ẖnt* – in ostraca many times written as *ẖnw* – which literally means “hide”. In two texts, O. DeM 769, 9[37] and O. DeM 924, 4, the word appears determined by  instead of . Moreover, in both instances it turns up in a series of garments, after *rwḏw*. Grandet translated both times “peau”, which is of course correct, but the determinatives as well as the context suggest that it was an item of dress, hence perhaps the leather loincloth.

The word *ẖnw* / *ẖnt* occurs many times in Deir el-Medîna texts; I have noted it in over twenty ostraca.[38] One wonders whether in more cases than the two mentioned above a hide made into a loincloth was meant, but without any indication, as for instance the determinative , this has to remain unknown.

Notes

1) In the literary ostracon O. DeM 1075, 8 *ꜥꜣt* occurs in an obscure context.
2) Between *ꜥꜣt* and the figure is written  *šbnt*, “various”. In O. DeM 85, 3 *šbn* occurs also there, without *t*, but with plural strokes.
3) Erichsen, *Demotisches Glossar*, 55.
4) Crum, *Coptic Dictionary*, 88a; Černý, *Coptic Etymological Dictionary*, 49.
5) Cf. von Deines-Westendorf, *Wörterbuch der medizinischen Texte*, I, 219 (“Leinenstoff”). See also Borghouts, *The Magical Texts of the Papyrus Leiden I 348*, p. 59, note 66.
6) Meeks, *Année lexicographique* 77.0570 and 78.0622 calls it “une qualité d’étoffe”, without specification. Grandet translates it in O. DeM 769 as “pièces de tissu”, also without stress on the material.

7) It looks almost like *ḥb-sd* !
8) O. Leipzig 3 (= *Hier. Ostr.* 33/1), 1 and 5; O. Ashmolean Museum 1945.39 (=*Hier. Ostr.*72/1), vs. 9; O. BM 50733 (+ O. Petrie 30 = *Hier. Ostr.* 19/2), vs. 4; O. Varille 13 (= O. Louvre E 27678: K*RI* VII, 238), 4. The last ostracon is depicted in *Les artistes de Pharaon*, nr. 155 (p. 205).
9) Perhaps on account of note 119 in *Commodity Prices*, 230-231.
10) McDowell, translating O. Ashmolean Museum 1945.39 (in *Village Life*, 34-35) rendered it as *inet*-garment, with a query mark.
11) Not quite clear, since the end of line 3 is broken off. The photograph in *Les artistes de Pharaon* (p. 205, nr. 155) shows that at present even more is lost than when Černý read it. However, 1 *snỉw* cannot be the price of the coffin; for that it is too low.
12) See, however, *Commodity Prices*, 288.
13) In 28, 3 written *bdnw*. See Gardiner, *Egyptian Hieratic Texts* (Leipzig, 1911), p. 13*, note 15.
14) It was probably not a loan-word but real Egyptian; cf. the review of Hoch's study by Ward, *CdE* 71 (1966), 27.
15) Hannig's *Grosses Handwörterbuch*, for instance, states (p. 255) that *bndw* is "e. Kleidungsstück (Gurt, Zeremonialschärpe)"; that is, a sash.
16) *n3* is here not the article but stands for *n*, as is clear in the love poem (see below), for in that text there is neither an *w* nor plural strokes after 𓃭. In this O. Gardiner 210 the 𓃭 too is superfluous after the 𓂋
17) Cf. Mathieu, *La poésie amoureuse*, pl. 19 bottom. The sentence runs: "I wiped (*sky.i*) my body with her *nfrwy*". Mathieu translates that (p. 100): "sa belle étoffe", referring to Paule Posener-Kriéger, *Les*

archives du temple funéraire de Néferirkarê-Kakaï, p. 364, where a type of cloth called *nfrw* is discussed. Hannig, *Grosses Handwörterbuch*, does not have the word in this spelling. He distinguishes between *nfrw*, "Kleid (der Götter)" and "Lumpen" (*nfry*). The latter is a nice euphemism!

18) In TT 45; see Davies-Gardiner, *Seven Private Tombs at Kurnah* (London, 1948), pl. IV, bottom right.

19) In O. DeM 255, 3; O. DeM 404, 3; O. Černý 15 (= *Hier. Ostr.* 61/3), vs. 17; O. Cairo 25723, 4.

20) That I have suggested in *Commodity Prices*, 291.

21) Kitchen calls this text "Payment to Pentaweret", but it is a laundry list, as the words of line 2: "(given) to the laundryman Pentaweret" show.

22) Černý noted that  seems to be a correction over the original .

23) In O. DeM 187, 4 simply *šndt*, in line 5 *šndt n ḳn*, "in perfect state". That *ḳn* occurs also in O. AG 116, 2 (K*RI* IV, 448), here as *m ḳn*.

24) The words *šndt mḥ* 1 are followed by a figure 20 in red. Does this indeed mean: 20 items?

25) I took it from Faulkner's *Concise Dictionary*, p. 270.

26) See above, p. 64.

27) For *ḫtmw* – usually translated as "seals" – see Grandet, *Le Papyrus Harris I*, vol. II, note 300.

28) Why Kitchen placed the fragment here, that is, in the time of Siptah-Twosre, is not clear.

29) *Pharaonic Egyptian Clothing*, p. 52.

30) It is preceded by *nfr.tw*; see above p. 65.

31) Note the ending *-ỉꜣ*; see above p. 16.

32) In Hannig's *Grosses Handwörterbuch*, p. 295, this word is noted, but with the remark that its existence is uncertain.

33) Cf. Jéquier, *Les frises d'objets des sarcophages du Moyen Empire* (Cairo, 1921), p. 6.

34) E.g. Gillian Vogelsang-Eastwood, *Pharaonic Egyptian Clothing*, 17-31; Rosalind Hall, *Egyptian Textiles*, 34-35.

35) Two in the British Museum: nrs. 2564 and 2199.

36) Another one, from the same tomb, formerly in the Field Museum of Natural History at Chicago, seems to be lost. For the pictures of them, see Vogelsang-Eastwood, *qp. śit.*, pls. 6 and 7.

37) Grandet transcribes , although the facsimile may suggest something else.

38) In O. DeM 551, 5, *h̲nt* (with ) is translated by Wente (*Letters*, nr. 173) as "goatskin". I fail to understand why it should be the hide of that particular animal. McDowell, *Village Life*, nr. 68B, translating the same text, renders it simply as "skin", and so did Wente himself in his translation of O. DeM 321, 2 (*nhy n h̲ny*, "a few skins"), in his *Letters*, nr. 253.

Chapter 5

Lists of Clothes

An important source for our knowledge about the daily dress in the workmen's community, quoted several times above, are those ostraca which contain a series of words for garments, in several instances each followed by a figure. I know 29 of these (see Table III at the end of this chapter), plus one papyrus with a similar list: Papyrus Turin Cat. $2104/_{223}$, II (unpublished).[1]

These texts are of various types. Some are evidently laundry lists, which in four instances is explicitly stated.[2] Others may also be so, although they do not contain the word *rḫtỉ*.[3] A fairly large number of ostraca are consisting completely or almost completely of words for clothes plus figures.[4] Others, however, are of a different type, e.g. O. DeM 769 ("List of the Garments of Tatuy?") or O. Brussels E 304 ("What was in the *pr-ḥḏ*").

A clear example of a laundry list is O. DeM 30, which records: "Year 1, III *prt* 15. This day, giving the garments to the laundrymen (*rḫtiw*). Coming (back) from him [*sic*] on III *prt* 16. What they had given to the riverbank, to launder", after which three lines of clothes.[5]

The beginning of O. DeM 258[6] is lost, but the first legible words are "[*rḫ*]*tỉw B3kỉ*". Further down are noted, at the beginning of the lines, the houses of some workmen ( plus a name), with after each various kinds of clothes, every time one, two or three items. In the last line we read: "What was given to the laundryman ….".

O. Berlin P 12649 (unpublished) begins, after the date III *prt* 16 (no year!), with *nty ỉw.w n p3 rḫtiw*, "Which are for (or: "what they [gave] to"?) the laundryman". The rest of the ostracon, five more lines, very irregularly spaced, contains words for garments, each with the figure "one" or "two". The whole gives the impression of a quickly scribbled note.

O. DeM 212, to take a less clear case, has at the top of col. I the name Khonsu, followed by four garments: 2 *dw*[7], 1 *sdỉ*, 1 *ẖnkỉ*, and 1 *ỉsh*. Under this comes the name Ḥay, followed in its turn by: 2 *dw*[7], 1 *ẖnkỉ*, and 1 *ỉsh*. On the top of this ostracon there is the remains of a line ….. *ẖnỉ* (no *k*). Of col. II the first three lines are erased, leaving in line 4 the name *ꜣny* and in line 5 *yny*, each followed by a blank spot. This is a good example to show our interpretation problems.

Simpler to understand is, for instance, O. DeM 90. It begins with: "Record (*mỉtt*) of the garments". These are then listed in lines 2 to 7. Or O. DeM 210, which consists of three columns of cloth names – in column 1, lines 1-3 are lost – each followed by a figure, except in col. III, line 1, where we find the date: IV *šmw* 17.

One ostracon, although recording mainly garments, is clearly not a laundry list. That is O. Turin 57061, in which four lines each record a single garment: *sḏy*, *rwḏw*, another *sḏy*, (all three of *nꜥꜥ*) and probably a second *rwḏw*. The first three are followed by a price in *deben*.[8] One could hesitate as to whether this can be called a list.

Yet another type of text is that of O. Varille 19 (unpublished). In col. I there are noted seven words for textiles[9] – two of them called *ỉswt*, "worn out" (see above p. 71) – in col. II three others, followed in line four by 4 pairs of sandals, and then a series of copper objects. This is continued in col. III, after which come wooden ones. That is: this is a list of all kinds of objects, an inventory of some sort – after each word a figure is written, mostly "one" or "two", but after the garments higher ones, up to 6 for the (good) *sḏwy* and even 9 for worn out ones. The garments are only one category of this list.

The question could be raised as to whether the garments in these lists are arranged in a more or less fixed order or not. If this would indeed be the case, it could perhaps help us to decipher badly legible traces, since we would know what to expect. In Table IV I have arranged the contents of thirteen ostraca, ignoring variations in spelling, e.g. those of *sḏw* or of *i͗sh*. I omitted from the table those lists that contain only very few names of garments (e.g. O. DeM 85, with only *sḏw* and *mss*), as well as those in which the order is not clear, e.g. O. DeM 404.[10]

One glance at the table makes it clear that there is not a rigorous order of all garments. Yet, a few points are conspicuous. *dꜣi͗w* (*dw*) is noted as the first one, except when, as happened in a few lists, *ḏꜣyt* is also mentioned, for that garment always precedes. Usually *sḏw* comes after *dꜣi͗w*, and *ḫnk* in the third place. This arrangement, *dꜣi͗w – sḏw – ḫnk*, we find five times; that of *dꜣi͗w – sḏw – rwḏw – ḫnk* four times.[11] Twice *pyr* is mentioned, both times at the end. *sd*, either with *n ḏrt* or with *pḥwy*, also comes rather low in the series, if it is recorded at all, which happens seldom. Altogether it seems that there existed a certain amount of regularity in the arrangements but it was far from strict.

Comparing these data with those from elsewhere, for instance, with the lists of garments in Pap. Harris I, it appears that there existed no general way of arranging words for garments (see Table V). Indeed, *dw* was most times number 1, except where *ḏꜣyt* occurs – in 14a, 12 this garment, here written , comes in the fourth place – but strangely enough when *dw* was not first it dropped to the third place. *i͗dg* and *mss* occur regularly lower in the series,[12] *šndy* still lower. Twice *dwy ḥry* follows directly *dw*, which seems logical, but once (in 14b) the two are separated by *sḏw*. The list of 63a, 14 – b, 4 is exceptional in that it is headed by *dw ḥry*, followed by *msst ꜥꜣt*. After these two, the order (*dw – sdw – i͗dg – hꜣwmn – msst – šndy*) seems fairly normal.

All we can say is that there is a slight tendency, as in ostraca, to arrange the various items in a fixed order, but the order of Pap. Harris I differs from that at Deir el-Medîna.

We can also compare the numbers of the various garments as noted in Papyrus Harris I with those known from the ostraca. However, the papyrus lists two series of clothes made of *sšr-nsw*, "royal linen", the highest quality, which does not occur in our Deir el- Medîna texts; possibly this type of linen cloth was too expensive for the workmen.[13] One could argue that garments made from this type of cloth should not be included in the comparison. Moreover, some items of dress mentioned in the Papyrus Harris I, although mostly in small numbers,[14] occur rarely or not at all in the Deir el-Medîna texts, where, on the other hand, clothes appear that are absent from the papyrus.[15]

Bringing together those figures that are comparable we get the following picture:

	DeM	**Harris**
dw	143	635
ḏ3yt	48	90
sḏw / sḏy	123	77
ỉdg	27	1509
mss	124	1697
hnk	35	2
ỉfd	58	44

Apart from these there are more garments recorded in Pap. Harris I, outside the lists: 150 *dw* (72, 15) and even 2968 *šndy*

(55b, 1). Other entries mention only "various garments" (*ḥbsw šbn*), sometimes in considerable quantities.[16] These we cannot compare with the evidence from the workmen's community.

However, the figures quoted above may give us an indication in which way the dress of the people in Deir el-Medîna agreed with or differed from that of those connected with the temples in the country. In the Village the number of *dw* is the highest, slightly higher than that of the *mss*; in the papyrus it is less than two-fifths of that, while the number of *mss* is the highest of all. Really surprising, however, is the number of *idg* in the Papyrus Harris: 1509; only slightly lower than that of *mss* (1697), while there occur only 27 in the texts of the workmen. On the other hand, at Deir el-Medîna the number of *sḏw* / *sḏy* (123) is about the same as those of *mss* (124), whereas in Pap. Harris I it is one of the lowest, even lower than that of *ḏȝyt*.

In other words, while at Deir el-Medîna *dw*, *mss* and *sḏw* / *sḏy* are the most common items of dress, in the Papyrus Harris these are *mss* and *idg*, at a distance followed by *dw*.[17] Also: the role of *idg* in the papyrus seems to be the same as that of *sḏw* / *sḏy* among the workmen. Yet, so far as we know, it was a completely different piece of dress.

Notes

1) The text is known to me from Černý's Notebook 23. Only col. II, 4-10 contains words for clothes; lines 11-13 list other things, as does col. III, except in line 9: *dw* 1 *ir.n dbn* 20.
2) O. DeM 30 and 258; O. Berlin P12649 (unpublished); O. Gardiner 193 (K*RI* VII, 311); for the latter cf. Chapter 4, note 21.

3) O. DeM 212; O. IFAO 1055 (unpublished). In these each time the name of a workman is followed by the mention of some garments. O. Turin 57464 may also belong to this category, but no names have here been left.

4) For some of them (O. DeM 86, II; 87; 88; 90). Valbelle suggets (*Les Ouvriers*, 284, note 3) that they too are laundry lists. After nr. 90 she adds: “etc. ....”; possibly she thought that this held also true for: O. DeM 211; 283; 404; 452; 583; 924; O. AG 110; O. IFAO 745; O. Gardiner 210 (the last three unpublished).

5) For a translation of this text, see Andrea McDowell, *Village Life*, nr. 32 (p. 60). On her next page are depicted some of Bruyère’s pictorial clothing ostraca (see Chapter 6).

6) Translated *op. cit.*, p. 59 (nr. 31).

7) Written almost as .

8) The price in the fourth line is replaced by a stroke.

9) In line 8: *ṯnfy*, “bag”; the others are clearly garments.

10) Should one here read horizontally (in each line two words) or from top to bottom the first words and then vertically the second words in each line? Probably the first method is correct. The same problem occurs in O. DeM 88 and O. DeM 583.

11) In O. DeM 452 preceded by *ḏ3yt* (written *i͗ḏ3*!).

12) For the couple *i͗dg* – *mss*, see above, *i͗dg*, p. 27.

13) In Pap. Harris I a few clothes of the quality *mk* are recorded, each time only one item: in total 3 *ḥbs* [sic] *šbn*. For *mk*, see above, p. 14, note 26. It occurs rarely and is therefore here ignored, as in the unique *šmꜥ nfr nfr* of 32b, 2.

14) *št3-ḥr* and *ẖnky*; also *h3mn* and *kḏmr*. For the last two, see Chapter 4.

15) *ish, pyr, mrw* and *rwḏw*. The last one does occur in Pap. Harris I, 18 b11 (31 items), but nowhere else. In view of its rather frequent appearance in Deir el Medîna texts this is conspicuous.

16) In 70b, 9 no less than 50877 (of all kinds of fabric).

17) Adding the 150 *dw* of 72, 15 to the 635 of the lists the total becomes 785. Then the number of *dw* would come near to half that of *mss*, and would be above the half of *idg*.

1)	O. DeM	30
2)	O. DeM	85
3)	O. DeM	86
4)	O. DeM	87
5)	O. DeM	88
6)	O. DeM	90
7)	O. DeM	210
8)	O. DeM	211
9)	O. DeM	212
10)	O. DeM	258
11)	O. DeM	283
12)	O. DeM	341
13)	O. DeM	404
14)	O. DeM	452
15)	O. DeM	583

16)	O. DeM	769
17)	O. DeM	865
18)	O. DeM	924
19)	O. AG	110
20)	O. Berlin	P 12649
21)	O. Brussels	E 304
22)	O. IFAO	745
23)	O. IFAO	1055
24)	O. Gardiner	193
25)	O. Gardiner	210
26)	O. Gardiner	265
27)	O. Turin	57061
28)	O. Turin	57464
29)	O. Varille	19
30)	Pap. Turin	$2104/_{223}$

TABLE III

The List of Garments

O. DeM	86, II	87	90	210		211	212		258			283[a)]	341	452	583	924	O. Varille 19
				II	III		Khonsu	Hay	6	7	8						
d3yt			1											1	1		1
d3iw (dw)	1	1	2		1	1	1	1		1	1	1	1	2	3	1	2
sḏw	2	2	3	1	2	2	2		1	2	2	2	2	3		2	3
rwḏw										3		6	5	4	6	3	
h̠nk	3	3		4	3	3	3	2		4		3	3	5		4	
mss				3								4					4
ish	5	4				4	4		2	5		5					
idg				2	2			3						7	4		
sd n ḏrt	6		4			5								8			
sd pḥ.wy		5				6			?					9			
iswt	7									6				10	2		
pyr	8											8					
	psḏw 4	*sd 6* *rrw 7*										*ifd 7*	*ifd 4*	*nṯr 6*			*ifd 5*

a) Rt. and vs. treated as one column

Table IV

The Order of the Various Garments

	A	B	C	D	E	F
	14a, 9 – 16	14b, 6 – 11	63a, 4 – 11	63a, 14 – b, 4	63b, 7 – 14	63b, 16 – c, 3
1	*dw*	*dw*	*dw*	*dw ḥry*	*t3 ḏ3it*	*t3 ḏ3it*
2	*dw ḥry*	*sḏw*	*dw ḥry*	*msst ʿ3t*	*sḏw*	*sḏw*
3	*h3wmn*	*dw ḥry*	*št3-Ḥr*	*dw*	*dw*	*dw*
4	*d3w*	*idg3*	*ḏ3iw*	*sḏw*	*idg*	*ifd*
5	*št3-Ḥr*	*msst*	*sḏw*	*idg*	*t3 mss*	*t3 msst*
6	*sḏw*	*šndy*	*ẖnky*	*h3wmn*	*ḳ3ḏ3 mr*	
7	*idg3*		*idg*	*msst*	*šndy*	
8	*msst*		*mss*	*šndy*	*ifd*	
	sšr-nsw	*šmʿ nfr*	*sšr-nsw*	*šmʿ nfr*	*šmʿ*	*nʿʿ*

TABLE V

The Lists of Papyrus Harris I

	A	B	C	D	E	F	Totals	
dw	37	2	17	234	218	1	509	635
dw ḥry	94	5	25	2			126	
h3mn	55			1			56	
ḏꜣwỉ	11		5		23	60	99	
štꜣ-Ḥr	2		3				5	
sḏw	1	4	30	29	1	12	77	
ỉdg	690	31	179	428	181		1509	
msst	489	29	168	399	43	567	1695	1697
msst ʿꜣt				2			2	
šndy		4		37	23		64	
ẖnky			2				2	
ḳḏmr					49		49	
ỉfd					40	4	44	
	sšr-nsw	*šmʿ nfr*	*sšr-nsw*	*šmʿ nfr*	*šmʿ*	*nʿʿ*	**4237**	

TABLE VI

The Number of Clothes in Papyrus Harris I

Chapter 6

Pictorial Clothing Lists

On a few Deir el-Medîna ostraca we find what look to be pictures of garments. The best known are published by Bruyère in his *Rapport sur les Fouilles de Deir el Médineh (1934-1935)*, Deuxième Partie: La nécropole de l'est (1937), p. 62 (fig. 32). The ostraca which show clothes – some depict pottery – are reprinted by Gillian Vogelsang-Eastwood in an article devoted to this subject in *GM* 128 (1992), 105-111. She identifies three of the garments: the triangular loincloth,[1] the bag-tunic, and the fringed shawl or sash.

In an article published shortly afterwards (*GM* 131, 1992, 55-60), I have suggested that these ostraca functioned as laundry lists, made by illiterate housewives. Within the various shapes there are dots, which could indicate the numbers of such clothes that went to the laundrymen.

There are some more of these ostraca than studied in these articles. Two of those Bruyère published he had already depicted in his first report of 1922-1923 (1924), p. 69, but there we find also a third one (figure a) which he left out of the later study. Rectangles of various shapes, one with fringes, also are found, together with pictures of sandals, on O. UC. 33252; see Anthea Page, *Ancient Egyptian Figured Ostraca* (Warminster, 1956), nr. 80 verso. The author explains these figures (p. 57) as being hieroglyphs; the rectangle with fringes representing Sign S32. That may be correct, in which case the rectangle without fringes could be explained as N37 (the garden pool). The presence of sandals, however, rather suggests items of dress.

Yet another ostracon of this type is O. Leipzig 1657 (now lost!), depicted and described by Emma Brunner-Traut in *Die altägyptische Scherbenbilder* (Wiesbaden, 1956), nr. 152 (p. 124 and pl. XLIV). Here we see a Bes-figure, a headrest, a dagger, and an uraeus, besides two rectangles and what could be a shawl. To each figure several strokes are noted, which seem to be the equivalent of the dots in other ostraca. The ostracon may well be a list of objects deposited in a tomb ("Grabbeigaben"), as Frau Brunner suggests. Whatever, the rectangles and the shawl seem to represent garments.

Notes

1) Note that fig. 2a looks larger than the rectangles on the same ostracon (her nr. 1 on p. 105). It also misses the line in the middle (the seam) that occurs in fig. 2b. The latter looks clearly like a loincloth. What the odd shape in ostracon 7 of fig. 1 () may represent is a mystery, as also are the round and oval shapes beside it.

Chapter 7

The Archaeological Evidence for Daily Dress

After dealing with the various words for garments which occur in the Deir el-Medîna texts we will now turn to the actual textile remains that have survived from the inhabitants of the Village, as well as to the representations of clothes on the tomb walls. The former may constitute the most important witnesses for what was really worn. However, even in the case of garments found in the tombs of the community one has to be cautious: were they indeed part of the daily dress, or were they perhaps especially made for the tomb?

Clothes of the workmen are mainly found in the tombs of the Eastern necropolis. Some are published by Bruyère in his report of the excavations of 1934-1935, part II (*La nécropole de l'est*), p. 58-63. Yet, these burials date from the Eighteenth Dynasty, whereas the large majority of the texts containing words for clothes are from the late Nineteenth and the Twentieth Dynasty. It seems unlikely that the normal dress of the workmen changed substantially over these years;[1] nevertheless, we have to be cautious.

The garments found by Bruyère are[2]:

1) a piece of cloth of 1.60 m. by 69 cm., possibly a woman's cloak;
2) a rectangular piece of cloth of 2 by 1 metres, which the excavator thought to be a sheet (*ifd*), afterwards developed into a woman's dress.
3) A bag-tunic.
4) Four triangular loincloths, one from a woman's burial, another – well washed – from that of a child.

Also from the Eighteenth Dynasty is the famous tomb of the chief workman Kha' (TT 8), discovered intact by Schiaparelli in 1906.[3] It contained several garments that are described and partly depicted in his report (p. 90-100).

They are: 50 triangular loincloths;
17 tunics;
2 "tovaglie": female wrap-around dresses (with fringes).[4]

With regards to the amounts we have to keep in mind that Kha' was certainly more prosperous than most of his workmen.

That the scenes of daily life in the Eighteenth Dynasty tombs, such as those representing banquets or fishing-and-fowling, possess a deeper, religious meaning is clear. It has recently again been argued by Lise Manniche in an article in *The Theban Necropolis. Past, Present and Future* (ed. by Nigel Strudwick and John H. Taylor, London 2003), 42-52.[5] That in itself does not mean that the way in which people are dressed in these scenes is unrealistic. Yet, it is obviously mainly "Sunday dress", and garments of the upper class. Moreover, underwear, if indeed this was worn, is of course not shown. But the main point is: these scenes which at first view seem to show us activities of daily life, actually mean the transformation of the dead. They carry a message, and how the people in them are dressed is irrelevant.

Moreover, such "realistic" scenes are rare to non-existent in later tombs. Of course, there too are people depicted, self-evidently dressed. The men almost always wear a kilt, the women a dress with fringes. However, there is no reason to suppose that these pictures present us reliable information about the costume of every day. That is: the tomb-pictures are not a good source for our present subject.

Notes

1) Cf. Vogelsang-Eastwood, *Pharaonic Egyptian Clothing*, p. 17: "…. there is no evidence as yet to suggest that short term fashion trends existed". It is unclear how short this "short term" in the conception of the author was, but it may well be that we have to think of periods longer than dynasties. That the Amarna Period in this respect constituted a break seems not likely.
2) See fig. 31 in Bruyère's report (p. 60).
3) Relazione sui lavori della missione archeologica italiana in Egitto (anni 1903-1920), Vol. Secondo: *La tomba intatta dell' architetto Cha nella necropoli di Tebe* (Torino, 1927).
4) These may be what the texts call *ỉfd*.
5) The title is revealing: "The *so-called* scenes of daily life in private tombs of the Eighteenth Dynasty" (italics mine).

Chapter 8

Footwear

To the daily dress belongs also what the people used to wear on their feet, if anything. The pictures in the tombs mostly show the Egyptians walking around barefoot,[1] but was that the reality?[2] One text at least offers sufficient reason to doubt it, namely Pap. Harris I. Both in 19b, 3 and 72, 12 we are told that no less than 15110 pairs of papyrus sandals were delivered to the Theban temples, and a few lines further on, in 19b, 11 and 73, 1, 3720 more leather sandals. Compared with the 150 *dw* garments (19b, 7 and 72, 15) that seems to be an enormous amount. Of course, we do not know for how many people they were intended; the leather ones perhaps mainly or exclusively for priests, the papyrus ones for the lower personnel. Anyhow, this text shows us that sandals were not rare.

Of course, in the ostraca from the relatively small community of necropolis workmen the numbers are lower than those for the personnel of the temples. Yet, once, in O. IFA0 827, 4 (unpublished), we find 1976 pairs recorded. Admittedly, all figures in this text – 66 loincloths (*sḏy*), 2166 sheets or nightdresses (*i͗fd*), and even 23200 *hi͗n* of honey – are surprisingly high. Since the first line of this ostracon is missing we cannot know what these figures mean; also not the large number of sandals.

Definitely lower, but still considerable, is the figure of 440 leather sandals in O. Ashmolean 1945.37 + .33, vs. 5 [+ O. Michaelides 90] (= *Hier. Ostr.* 75).[3] In this text too the numbers are rather high, e.g. 20,000 *ḥḳ3t* of grain, or – more in the sphere of this study – 424 various garments (*ḥbsw šbn*).

Still lower is the figure in the Giornale dell'anno 3, I, 4[4]: 60 pairs of sandals. In all other texts from Deir el-Medîna there are mentioned less than ten; mostly one or two, but in O. Cairo

25583, 2 four and in O. Cairo 25677, 18 seven. Yet, I have found 133 ostraca in which sandals occur in 188 entries. Moreover, they are mentioned in nine papyri from the Village. Among these is even one short papyrus which deals exclusively with these objects, viz. Pap. DeM 31. The same is the case with two ostraca: O. DeM 240 and 241. They together demonstrate that sandals were certainly not rare in this community.[5]

In order to give an impression of the way in which they occur in our material I present here translations of these three text

O. DeM 240[a]

1. …. Sandals which are with the draughtsman Nebre‘.
2. Women's [sandals], 3 pairs, were put in the palanquin.
3. Large men's sandals, 2 pairs, were in the box.
4. Men's sandals, given from Pharaoh (l.p.h.)[b], 5 pairs; Inynakhte brought the documents.
5. Sandals put aside to be stitched: single sandals, 19.
6. Men's sandals given to the scribe Re‘mose: 1 pair.
7. Men's sandals given to Pendwau: 1 pair.
8. Sandals which the sandalmaker Ma‘ḥy made: 9 various pairs of sandals, being [18] san[dals].
9. Sandals which the sandalmaker Kha‘u made: 8 pairs of sandals.
10. [Sandals] given from Pharaoh (l.p.h.)[b]: 2 pairs. The 2 are for Re‘ḥotpe.
11. ……..

Vs.[c] 1. Their commissions which are with the scribe Pa[y]:
2. Giving one to Pre‘emḥab ….
3. Giving one in order to bring [to?][d] Patjarbu: 2 [*sic*]
4. One to put on the feet (??).
5. Together, which are with the scribe Pa[y]: 4.
6. One for Ḥuy.

a. According to the names dating from the early years of Ramesses II.
b. For this expression, see below, p. 101.
c. The verso is translated by Cooney in *Living and Writing in Deir el-Medine* (ed. Andreas Dorn and Tobias Hofmann, Basel, 2006), p. 49.
d. So Cooney – but without “to” – disregarding  after . Could this mean *in-ḫt*, “woodcutter”?

O. DeM 241[a]

1. Record[b] of the wood ….

2. …. gave Re'mery to the carpenter

3. Minkhew[c]:

makes 1 [*khar*].

4. a balance,

5. 3 *deben* of copper

6. ……..[d]

Vs. 1…. sandals, makes[e] 2 [sc. *khar*].

2. women's sandals, makes 1 [*khar*].

3.sandals,

4. women's sandals, makes 1 *oipe*.

5. women's sandals, makes 1 *oipe*.

6. sandals, makes 1 *oipe*.

7. onions, makes 1 [*khar*].

8.1 *hin* of *mrḥt*-oil.[f]

9. …..

a. For the date, Ramesses III to IV, see my *Commodity Prices*, p. 45.
b. *r rdit rḫtw*. For the translation "list", see *Commodity Prices*, p. 497. However, since not a plural (*ꜣḫt nb*) follows, but *pꜣ ḫt*, a slightly different translation is required. What is lost at the end of the line is not clear.
c. Benedict Davies, *Who's Who at Deir el-Medina*, 189, suggests that the two men (he calls the first one Meryre') were brothers, sons of Ḥori (III).
d. Only the signs □ were legible to Černý.
e. For *ir n*, see *Commodity Prices*, 9, note 20. Graefe explained this (*FS Elmar Edel*, Bamberg, 1979, p. 174) as *ir*(*w*) *n*, "made to".
f. For *mrḥt*, cf. *Commodity Prices*, 335 ff.

Commentary

Clearly each entry of the verso, line 1-6, lists one pair of sandals, with its price.

Pap. DeM 31[a]

1. ….[b] the necropolis. As soon as my letter reaches you, you shall try to acquire the sandals.
2. …. one pair of leather enveloping men's sandals; one pair of leather sandals of a priest; one pair of leather sandals;
3. …. one pair of leather enveloping men's sandals.[c] He said: I'll get [them] for him from ….[d]
4. …. . He let me bring one [pair of] leather sandal soles,
5. [and I] brought it[e] to him. He did not [give] anything for it.[e] He let bring
6. …. my enveloping [sandals]. Nothing was given to me for it. Sandals ….
7. …. and [he] let me bring his leather sandals ….

a. Published by Černý, *Papyrus hiératiques de Deir el-Médineh*, II (= Doc. de Fouilles, Tome 22, 1986), pl. 21. Translated by Wente, *Letters from Ancient Egypt* (Atlanta, 1990), Nr. 262.
b. Some words are lost at the beginnings of the lines and at the end of the letter.
c. The same entry as the line above, but here 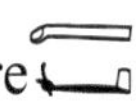, the determinative of *ꜥfnw*, is missing.
d. Wente suggested "the sandalmaker", but I fail to see on what grounds.

e. *.f*, "the pair". In English we are inclined to refer to a pair of sandals in the plural ("them"); so translates Wente.

Commentary

What exactly is described in this letter is not clear, mainly due to the losses at the beginnings of the lines. So much is certain: sandals constituted a common good.

The word for sandals in these texts is *twt*,[6] which is written in many ways. The first sign is always , which can be followed by . The writing for a *t* is of course common; *wt* is written as or , a variant being . The determinative is either one or two signs of sandals. The most frequent forms are and or . However, in many instances there is added *rdwy*, "two feet", either fully written ( ), or abbreviated (to). In the last instance one could surmise that the legs are merely a second group of determinatives – that is, not pronounced – and the addition could then be a misinterpretation by the scribe. That is not correct, for there are also instances where , or even , precedes *twt*, sometimes connected with *twt* by *n* (e.g. O. DeM 115, 4-5, or O. Gardiner 279, 3, unpublished). Once we find even the form (O. DeM 295, I, 8), Clearly, *rd.wy* was pronounced.[7]

There is one more distinction between *twt* alone and *rdwy* (*n*) *twt*. In a few texts these words are accompanied by the article. The word *twt* is then preceded by *nꜣ*,[8] whereas *rd.wy* (*n*) *twt* has *p3*.[9] I have found only one instance of *wʿ n rd.wy n twt*, viz. O. DeM 554, 7-8. Evidently, *twt* alone was felt to be a plural, *rd.wy n twt* as singular.

The word *twt*, in whatever way written, is actually the dual of *ṯbw*, "sole.[10] By its very nature this word occurs rarely in the ostraca; sandals occur almost always in pairs.[11] The word "pair" (, ʿ) is not always written. For instance, in O. DeM 241 vs. (see above) it is omitted, although clearly pairs of sandals are meant.

In many instances in the Deir el-Medîna texts there is indicated whether the sandals are of a man or of a woman. Yet, there seems to be no clear difference in shape between them. "Men's sandals" are called *twt ʿḥ3wty* or, seldom, *twt ṯ3y*,[12] but in many instances only the sign follows the word *twt*. I know of 38 cases of such sandals of a man, while in 26 instances they are said to be of a woman, either *twt* or or .[13]

Whereas in Pap. Harris I over 15,000 pairs of sandals of papyrus (*ḏmʿ*) are recorded (see above), as against over 3700 of leather, which would create the impression that papyrus sandals were normal and leather ones more rare,[14] the picture from the ostraca is the opposite. I found only two instances where they are said to be of papyrus,[15] as against 37 in which leather is said to be their material.[16] This can be fully written out as (*dḥr*, "leather"),[17] but is mostly only indicated by the sign as the determinative of twt. It is usually written directly after , before other additions such as ;[18] in one text it occurs even instead of these sandal-signs.[19]

In three texts the sandals are called (*n*) *Pr-ʿ3*,[20] while in O. DeM 240, 4 and 10 (see above) they are said to be *rdyt m Pr-ʿ3*.[21] The two of line 10 are for a Reʿḥotep. It is not clear whether it is of importance that this text dates from the reign of Ramesses II, hence rather early. Does the mention that sandals are "of" or "from" Pharaoh mean that they belong to the provisions distributed irregularly among the workmen, the so-called *mkw*? These consisted mostly of raw materials,[22] but also of garments;[23] nowhere, however, so far as I know, of sandals. Are the few references to Pharaoh's sandals sufficient proof that this type of footwear was sometimes included in the distribution?

One type of footwear occurring in the New Kingdom deserves a more fundamental discussion. The normal Egyptian sandal consists of a sole and two straps; one passing over the instep; the other, longitudinal, fixed near the top and, passing between the toes, goes up and is fastened at the first one.[24] Carla Alfano, who wrote a special study on Egyptian sandals,[25] distinguishes four types of straps, but the differences are not reflected in the language. However, there was one variation which has its own name: the *twt ꜥfnw*, "enveloping sandals". It is depicted in some Theban tombs, e.g. that of Rekhmireꜥ (TT 100), in which on the wall there is a representation of four rows of sandals, the third one from the top being the enveloping type;[26] or that of the vizier Useramun (TT 61), where the old vizier Aamethu is shown wearing them;[27] or that of Tjanuni, where Mutiri, Tjanuni's wife, wears such sandals.[28] Actual footwear of this type was found in the tomb of Yuia and Thuiu (KV 46),[29] as well as once in tomb 1069 at Deir el-Medîna (Rapport DeM 1926, 35: "chaussure avec claque et lacets de cuir").

The word *twt ꜥfnw* occurs in some Deir el-Medîna texts, viz. O. BM 29560 (= *Hier. Ostr.* 85/1), vs. 16; O. DeM 213, 6; Pap. DeM 31, 2 (see above). Also in Pap. Turin 1907/8, II, 3 (*JEꜣ* 52, 1966, pl. XVI), but that is probably not from the Village. It is in so far of interest that it is stated to be of a woman, which is perhaps also the case in the first ostracon;[30]

the other two are certainly of a man. Hence, both men and women could wear such sandals.[31]

This may be the correct place to add a note to another word. In O. Gardiner 162, 8 (K*RI* VII, 310) there occur, among the objects of a transaction between a workman and a chief policeman, three . The same words seem to be meant in O. Turin 57480, 6, although here *twt* is almost fully lost.[32] A third instance may be Pap. Turin 1880 (the Turin Strike Papyrus), vs. 5, 18 (*R3ḏ* 48), where  appears before *twt*. In my *Commodity Prices*, p. 298, I translated this *sfẖ* as "thongs"[33] (I would now say "straps"). Yet, the verb *sfẖ*, from which it seems to be derived, means "to loosen, to remove, to discard".[34] Sturtewagen, in *Studies in Egyptology* (FS for Miriam Lichtheim), vol. II, p. 939, discussed the place in the Turin Strike Papyrus, partly following Wente's discussion in his *Late Ramesside Letters*, p. 53. Sturtewagen interpreted it as "remnant, a pair of sandals", that is, "a pair of used sandals", Whether that agrees with the the price in O. Turin 57480, which is 1 *deben*, not lower,[35] and with its function as part of a transaction in O. Gardiner 162, is not clear. I have to confess that I am not fully convinced, but that  means "thongs" = "straps" seems not anymore certain.[36]

Notes

1) I have found representations of sandals only in the following Deir el-Medîna tombs:

    TT6 (Neferhotep I and Nebnofer): both men when adoring deities, but not their wives.
    TT 217 (Ipuy): men adoring and being honoured; not their wives.

TT 267 (Ḥay): Ḥay and a priest, perhaps also the wife of Ḥay.

TT 338 (May): priests offering.

TT 359 (Anḥerkhew II): several men, but also King Amenhotep I and Queen Ahmose Nefertari.

In other tombs, e.g. TT 1, 2, 3, 5 and 8, so far as I know, no sandals are depicted. However, feet are low on the wall, where painting is easily lost, and the photograph's in Bruyère's report are not at all clear.

2) One possibility was expressed by Hayes in *The Scepter of Egypt*, vol. I, p. 109: "Sandals were probably worn only on formal occasions". Yet I doubt whether this is quite correct.
3) Translated by Allam, *Hieratische Ostraka und Papyri*, Nr. 3 (p. 20-22).
4) G. Botti and T.E. Peet, *Il giornale della necropolis di Tebe* (Turin, 1928), pl. 50.
5) Of course, sandals are also mentioned in literary texts, e.g. Pap. Lansing 9, 10; Pap. Anastasi III, 6, 8; Pap. Anastasi IIIA, 6-7; Pap. Anastasi V, 23, 1; Pap. Sallier I, 7, 4, etc.
6) Grandet, in the indexes to vols. 8, 9, and 10 of the *Catalogue des ostraca hiératiques non littéraires*, transcribes *tjw.t*; that is, *tj* for the sign , also where no  follows. Yet, the singular is *tbt* or *ṯbt*; the latter, probably indeed pronounced with *tj*, is nevertheless nowhere written with . In his glossary to Pap. Harris I (vol. 3 of his publication), p. 195, Grandet transcribes *tbwty*, also when no  is written (19b, 3 and 11). All this is not very clear, but the evidence is indeed confusing.

7) Grandet transcribes *tjw.ty rd.wy* (e.g. in O. DeM 10044, vs. 2 and O. DeM 10070, 2), translating it as “semelles de sandals”. Hence, he interprets *rd.wy* as “soles”, not as “feet”. I admit, “feet-sandals” does not sound very convincing, but is “soles of sandals” so much better? Were so many times indeed sandals without straps, soles only being indicated?
8) O. Gardiner 64 (= *Hier. Ostr.* 49/2), 7; O. DeM 446, 9; Pap. Turin 1879 (= K*RI* VI, 335), vs. I, 7.
9) O. DeM 115, 4-5; O. Cairo 25588, 13; O. Cairo 25597, 6; O. Gardiner 147, 1-2 (unpublished). In one ostracon from the Valley of the Queens (Koenig, *BIFAO* 88, p. 119), Doc. V, vs. 3: *p3 ꜥ n twt*.
10) Hence it is sometimes written . That the *b* was dropped in the pronounciation appears evident from Demotic *tw* and Coptic **ⲧⲟⲟⲩⲉ**; cf. Černý, *Coptic Etymological Dictionary*, p. 199.
11) An exception could be O. Louvre E 3263 (= *Hier. Ostr.* 65/2), vs. 2: , but the last sign is not certain. In O. Glasgow D 1925.72 (= O. Colin Campbell 7) + O. Leipzig 18, 4 is perhaps  written, but the determinative looks more like ; moreover  follows. In the Giornale dell’anno 3, 4 (see above, note 4) we read: “left, 1 pair of , 60” which seems impossible. Perhaps simply “60 pairs of sandals” was meant. The writing of *ṯbw* is not clear.
12) Known to me only from O. DeM 289, 3 and O. Cairo 25677, 18.
13) In O. Černý 15 (= *Hier. Ostr.* 61/3), II, 3: *twt n st-ḥmt ꜥ* 1 (with *n*!); in vs. 19 a pair is called *twt ꜥḥ3* () *r* (!) *st*, “man’s sandals for a woman”.

14) This is in contrast to the real objects discovered by Bruyère in the course of his excavations: almost 50 of leather as against less than 10 of papyrus, dompalm leaves, alpha grass, etc. Is that because leather is more durable?
15) O. DeM 115, 5-6 and O. Cairo 25679, 8.
16) For leather sandals, see Helck, *Materialien zur Wirtschaftsgeschichte* V, 940 ff. (with an addition on p. 1021 of vol. VI). Unfortunately, this list contains mistakes and is incomplete.
17) In O. Desroches 5, 9 (unpublished): *rd.wy n twt* () *m*  (with *m*!).
18) E.g. O. Nash 3 (= O. BM 65935 = *Hier. Ostr.* 56/2), 6.
19) O. Louvre E 3263 (= *Hier. Ostr.* 65/2), vs. 4 ().
20) O. Nash 3, 5 (see note 18); O. DeM 215, 6; O. Berlin 12647, 4. The last instance is less certain, for the word *twt* is lost at the beginning of the line.
21) Cf. the garments said to be *n Pr -ʿꜣ*; see above p. 12.
22) In Pap. Turin 1881, IV, 11 (K*RI* VI, 613): 24 hides (for footwear?).
23) O. Cairo 25504, vs. I, 4 (80 *ḥbsw*); Pap. Turin 1881, III, 4 (K*RI* VI, 612): 58 *mss*, and in IV, 10 (K*RI* VI, 613): 95 *ḥbsw*.
24) See e.g. fig. 104 in Hayes, *The Scepter of Egypt*, vol. II, p. 188.
25) Carlo Alano, *I sandali: moda e rituale nell'antico Egitto* (Città di Castello, 1987).
26) Norman de Garis Davies, *The Tomb of Rekh-mi-Reʿ at Thebes*, vol. II, pl. LIV (bottom right).
27) Eberhard Dziobek, *Die Gräber des Vezirs User-Amun. Theben Nr. 61 und 131*, pl. 81.
28) Annelies und Artur Brack, *Das Grab des Tjanuni. Theban Nr. 74*, pl. 3.

29) Theodore M. Davis, *The Tomb of Iouiya and Touiyou*, pl. XLIV (right hand pair).
30) It is worn by Mutiri in the tomb of Tjanuni.
31) The "child's shoe" on the photograph in Frankfort – Pendlebury, *The City of Akhenaten*, II, pl. 35, 4 (see also p. 23) is of quite a different type! Whether this was also called *ʿfnw* is uncertain.
32) Lopez restored it between brackets, and Černý had originally suggested it.
33) It was accepted in Lesko's *Dictionary of Late Egyptian*, vol. III, p. 43.
34) Cf. the use of *sfẖ* with *ẖ3w*, "tool", in O. Cairo 25798, 3; Pap. Geneva MAH 15274, vs. I, 1 (K*RI* VI, 144); Weight 5132. See above p. 10.
35) Cf. Table L in *Commodity Pri*ces, pp. 294-295.
36) On Middle Kingdom coffins the expression *sfẖ nmtt* occurs, which Jéquier, *Les frises d'objets* (*MIFAO* 47, Cairo 1921), 28, translates "lien pour la marche". That is said of sandals. Is this an indication as to its meaning?

Bibliography

C. Alfano, *I sandali: moda e rituale nell'antico Egitto* (Città di Castello, 1987)

S. Allam, *Hieratische Ostraka und Papyri aus der Ramessidenzeit* (Tübingen 1973)

Les artistes de Pharaon, à Deir el Medineh et la Vallée des Roi (cat. Expositions in the Louvre, in Brussels as in Turin, 2002-2003)

J. F.Borghouts, *The Magical Texts of the Papyrus Leiden I* 348, (Leiden 1971)

G. Botti e T. E. Peet, *Il giornale della necropolis di Tebe* (Toriono 1971)

A. Brack, A. Brack, *Das Grab des Tjanuni. Theban Nr. 74(*Mainz am Rhein 1977)

E. Brunner-Traut, *Die altägyptische Scherbenbilder* (Wiesbaden, 1956)

B. Bruyère, *Rapport sur les Fouilles de Deir el Médineh (1934-1935)*, Deuxième Partie: La nécropole de l'est (Le Caire 1937)

B. Bruyère, *Tombes thébaines de Deir el Médineh à décoration monochrome* (Le Caire, 1952)

R. A. Caminos, *Late-Egyptian Miscellanies*, (London 1954)

R. A. Caminos, *Literary Fragments in Hieratic Script* (Oxford, 1956)

J. Černý, *Coptic Etymological Dictionary* (Cambridge 1976)

J. Černý, *Hieratic Inscriptions from the Tomb of Tut'ankhamūn* (Oxford, 1965)

J. Černý, *Late Ramesside Letters* (Bruxelles 1939)

J. Černý, *Pap. hiératiques de Deir el-Médineh* (2 vols, Cairo, 1978 and 1986)

J. Černý and A. H. Gardiner, *Hieratic Ostraca* (Oxford, 1957)

W. E. Crum, *Coptic Dictionary* (Oxford 1939)

B. G. Davies, *Who's who at Deir el-Medina: a prosopographic study of the royal workmen's community* (Leiden 1999)

N. de G. Davies, Seven Private Tombs at Kurnah, Ed/ by A.H. Gardiner (London, 1948)

N. de G. Davies, *The Tomb of Rekh-mi-Re' at Thebes*, (2 vols., New York 1943)

W. V. Davies (ed.). *Colour and Painting in Ancient Egypt* (London, 2001)
Th. M. Davis, *The Tomb of Iouiya and Touiyou* (London 1907)
H. von Deines, W. Westendorf, *Wörterbuch der medizinischen Texte*, (2 vols., Berlin 1961-1962)
A. Dorn and T. Hofmann (editors), *Living and Writing in Deir el-Medine* (Basel, 2006)
E. Dziobek, *Die Gräber des Vezirs User-Amun. Theben Nr. 61 und 131* (Mainz am Rhein 1994)
Egypt's Golden Age: The Art of Living in the New Kingdom (Boston, 1982)
M. Görg, E. Pusch, *Festschrift Elmar Edel:* 12. März 1979, Bamberg, 1979
W. Erichsen, *Demotisches Glossar, (*Milanoagen 1954)
R. O. Faulkner, *The Ancient Egyptian Coffin Texts*, (3 vols, Warminster 1973)
R. O. Faulkner, *A Concise Dictionary of Middle Egyptian* (Oxford 1962)
O. Firchow, *Ägyptologische Studien* (=Festschrift Grapow) (Berlin, 1955)
H. W. Fischer-Elfert, *Die satirische Streitschrift des Papyrus Anastasi I* (Würzburg 1983)
H. Frankfort and J. D. S. Pendlebury, *The City of Akhenaten, Pt. 2 , The Excavations at Tell El Amarna during the seasons 1926-1932* (London, 1933)
A. Gardiner, *Egyptian Hieratic Texts*, Part I (Hildesheim 1964)
A. Gardiner, *Hieratic Papyri in the British Museum.Third Series*: *Chester Beatty Gift* (2 vols., London 1935)
A. Gardiner, *Ramesside Administrative Documents* (Oxford, 1995)
R. Germer, *Die Textilfärberei und die Verwendung gefärbter Textilien im Alten Ägypten* (Wiesbaden, 1992)
M. Goecke-Bauer in our *Woodcutters, Potters and Doorkeepers*, (Leiden, 2003)
P. Grandet, *Catalogue des ostraca hiératiques non littéraires*, Tome IX, nos. 831-1000 (Cairo 2003)
P. Grandet, *Le Papyrus Harris I*, (BM 9999) (2 vols., Le Caire, 1999)

I. Grumach, *Untersuchungen zur Lebenslehre des Amenemope* (München, Berlin, 1972)

M. Gutgesell, *Die Datierung der Ostraka und Papyri aus Deir el-Medineh* (2 vols., Hildesheim 1983- 2002)

R. Hall, *Egyptian Textiles* (Aylesbury 1986)

R. Hannig, *Grosses Handwörterbuch Ägyptisch-Deutsch* (2800-950 v. Chr.) (Mainz 1995)

W. C. Hayes, *The Scepter of Egypt* (2 Vols., Cambridge, Mass 1953-1959)

W. Helck, *Die Beziehungen Ägyptens zu Vorderasien im 3. und 2. Jahrtausend* (Wiesbaden, 1960)

W. Helck, *Materialien zur Wirtschaftsgeschichte des Neuen Reiches* (6 vols, Wiesbaden 1961-1969)

J. E. Hoch, *Semitic Words in Egyptian texts of the New Kingdom and Third Intermediate Period* (Princeton 1994)

S. Israelit-Groll (ed), *Studies in Egyptology presented to Miriam Lichtheim* (2 vols, Jerusalem, 1990)

J. J. Janssen, *Commodity Prices of the Ramessid period : an economic study of the village of necropolis workmen at Thebes* (Leiden 1975)

J. J. Janssen, *Two Ancient Egyptian Ship's Logs* (Leiden, 1961)

J. J. Janssen, E. Frood, and M. Goecke-Bauer, *Woodcutters, Potters and Doorkeepers* (Leiden, 2003)

G. Jéquier, *Les frises d'objets des sarcophages du Moyen Empire* (Cairo, 1921)

B. Kemp, G. Vogelsang-Eastwood, *The Ancient Textile Industry at Amarna,* (London, 2001)

K. A. Kitchen, *Ramesside Inscriptions, Historical and Biographical* (8 vols, Oxford, 1975-1990)

K*RI*, see Kitchen, *Ramesside Inscriptions*

L. H. Lesko, B. Switlaski, *A Dictionary of Late Egyptian* (5 vols., Berkeley, California, 1982-1990)

M. Lichtheim, *Ancient Egyptian Literature* (3 vols., Berkely, 1973-1980)

B. Mathieu, *La poésie amoureuse de l'Égypte ancienne* (Cairo, 1966)

C. Maystre, *La tombe de Nebenmât* (Le Caire, 1930)

A. G. McDowell, *Village Life: laundry lists and love songs* (Oxford 1999)

D. Meeks, *Année lexicographique I-III,* (3 vols., Paris 1980-82)
M. Müller, *Die Liebespoesie der Alten Ägypter* (Leipzig, 1899)
P. Nicholson and I. Shaw (editors), *Ancient Egyptian Materials and Technology* (Cambridge, 2000)
H. Otten, E. Akurgal, etc. (editors), *Hittite and other Anatolian and Near Eastern studies in honour of Sedat Alp: Sedat Alp'a armağan: Festschrift für Sedat Alp (*Ankara 1992)
A. Page, *Ancient Egyptian Figured Ostraca in the Petrie Collection* (Warminster, 1956)
A. J. Peden, *The Reign of Ramesses IV* (Warminster 1994)
T.E. Peet, *Il giornale della necropolis di Tebe* (Turin, 1928)
T. E. Peet, *The Great Tomb-robberies of the Twentieth Egyptian Dynasty* (Oxford 1930)
P. Posener-Kriéger, *Les archives du temple funéraire de Néferirkarê-Kakaï (Les papyri a'Abousir)* (Cairo, 1976)
R*AD*, see Gardiner, *Ramesside Administrative Documents*
E. Schiaparelli, *La tomba intatta dell' architetto Cha nella necropoli di Tebe* (Turin, 1927)
N. Strudwick and J. H. Taylor (editors), *The Theban Necropolis. Past, Present and Future* (London, 2003)
M. Tosi, M. T. Nicola, *Vita quotidiana nel villaggio operaio di Deir El Medina da ostraca Iscritti e figurati* (Imola, 2003)
D. Valbelle, *Catalogue des poid*s *à inscriptions hiératiques de Deir el-Médineh* (Cairo, 1977)
D. Valbelle, *Les ouvriers de la tombe: Deir-el-Médineh à l'époque* (Cairo 1985)
J. Vandier, *La tombe de Nefer-Abou* (Cairo, 1935)
G. Vogelsang-Eastwood, *Pharaonic Egyptian Clothing* (Leiden, 1993)
E. F. Wente*,* *Late Ramesside Letters* (Chicago, 1967)
E. F. Wente, *Letters from Ancient Egypt* (Atlanta, 1990)
Wimmer, *Hieratische Paläographie der nicht-literarischen Ostraka der 19. und 20. Dynastie*, (2 vols., Wiesbaden 1995)